KEELE'S TEMPLAR WINDOW

And the Templars

JACQUES DE MOLAY & THOMAS TOTTY

Robin Studd

North Staffordshire Press

Newcastle-under-Lyme

Staffordshire

Keele's Templar Window And the Templars Jacques de Molay & Thomas Totty

ISBN 978-1-9998703-7-9

Published in 2018

North Staffordshire Press

10 Queen Street

Newcastle-under-Lyme

ST5 1ED

CONTENTS

ILLUSTRATIONS

Photographs are by the author and Samuel Winter

PREFACE

Keele's parish church, dedicated to St John the Baptist, is a nineteenth-century replacement of its medieval predecessor, but the medieval window within it, which was preserved when the church was rebuilt in 1868 has been completely overlooked.

This monograph is, therefore, concerned with the history of a window and the medieval window glass within it, whose significance has become apparent only very recently. It would be a cliché to say that this has been a voyage of discovery, but the fact is that at each stage of the research undertaken new revelations of the significance of the content of Keele's medieval window have demonstrated not just that it is of local importance, but that it contributes to our understanding of medieval European history. It concerns both the history of the later crusades and also the fortunes and fate of the Knights Templar.

Keele's nineteenth century window glass is of high quality and sufficiently distinguished in its own right to be listed. It is a fine example of the work of the firm

Clayton and Bell and has been influenced by developments in the glazier's art in the medieval period. Impressive as the nineteenth-century glass is, however, it is not to be discussed here.

Unlocking the content of the medieval window and trying to discover its meaning and significance is, however, the object of this essay.

The window has been known to me for the past fifty years but like others living, working and serving the community at Keele, I largely ignored it and contented myself with the general opinion that the contents of the window were a confused jumble of broken pieces of medieval glass unamenable to rational explanation. It was reassuring that those who had arrived at a grade II* listing for the church at large had said it all by ignoring the window and its glass. That was, until I did what any self-respecting medieval historian should have done and spent more than a few seconds contemplating the window carefully and trying to interrogate its meaning. When my wife became churchwarden of Keele, I seized my chance to sit and stare at the glass, and to ask questions, because the church stands alone on a hill, and can seem rather remote, especially on winter evenings, it was desirable that somebody should accompany her when she was carrying out her wardenial duties. It did not take very long to realise that the dismissive view that the window glass was a confusing muddle did not suffice. What initially had been a puzzle, became a challenge requiring both detective work and patience.

What follows is really an interim report on my findings because, I am confident that there is more to be discovered.

Starting was easy, because in 1985 I was asked by Dr Christopher Harrison to contribute to a series of local history talks at Keele University which were published by the University in the following year as *Essays in the History of Keele*, ed. C.J. Harrison.

My contribution to the collection was an essay entitled 'A Templar Colony in North Staffordshire: Keele before the Sneyds', which tried to put into perspective the part played by 'the poor fellow soldiers of Christ and of The Temple of Solomon', otherwise known as The

Templars, in the history of Keele. Keele, we learned, stood at the centre of a group of acquisitions and benefactions to the Templar Order from the twelfth century, and was the only house of this subscription within Staffordshire. As a Templar foundation, it subsumed the privileges of its Order, making it exempt from the intervention of the bishop of Lichfield and his officials, and that gave tenants on the manor an ability to self-govern, which was not generally found elsewhere.

The parish boundary was marked by a series of crosses patées defining the privileged area; a parish guild dedicated to the Blessed Virgin Mary, to which parishioners were expected to contribute four pence a year, existed from at least the thirteenth century, and the guild paid for the chaplain. Life on a Templar manor, with its protective ecclesiastical status, was attractive to migrants in the thirteenth century who provided the necessary labour force to enable it to take in areas of uncleared woodland, and so to thrive, as can be evidenced by the extant manorial accounts. Four common fields, a slight variation on the common three-field system found elsewhere, operated in the manor at Keele from the twelfth century, producing principally oats, which were better suited to the weather conditions in this quasi-upland location, but also to produce fodder, bread, oatmeal and, of course, oatcakes. Sizeable flocks of sheep, draught animals

[Fig.1: Knights Templar church at Famagusta, Cyprus: the cross patée signifies the exempt status of this building.]

appropriate to its woodland environment and a coalmine contributed to medieval Keele's economic well-being until the downturn in the medieval economy at the beginning of the fourteenth century.

Dramatic disruption and change came to Keele's residents after 1307 when, first, the Templars present were arrested and imprisoned, and second, the mighty lord of Newcastle-under-Lyme, the earl of Lancaster of the day, claimed Keele as his own, and third, the Knights Hospitaller acquired the manor.

Having set out the broad outlines of a general history of the manor until the early fourteenth century I next sought to join in a debate on the effect of the suppression of the Templars at Keele by publishing an account of the fortunes of the one Templar brother who was present at Keele when the sheriff's officers arrived to confiscate the manor in 1308[1]. Ralph Tanet started this phase of his life as a sergeant-custodian of the manor, then as preceptor of Keele, and ended it by

---

1 R. Studd, 'From Preceptor to Prisoner of the Church: Ralph Tanet of Keele and the Last of the Templars', *Staffordshire Studies* 8 (1996), 36-49. The article understates the position of Thomas Totty of Thoraldeby.

being made a prisoner of the church and ordered by the Inquisition to live under the authority of the bishop of Norwich. Although this was largely based upon the selective Latin text available in *Councils and Synods*, ii, ed. F.M. Powicke and C. Cheney (1964), it is only with the publication of the full text, with translation by Professor Nicholson, *The Proceedings Against the Templars in the British Isles*, 2 volumes (2011), that it has become possible to discover the detail of individual brethren brought before the Inquisition, and to outline Keele's significant role in those events.

This monograph could not have been written without Professor Helen Nicholson's remarkable, and invaluable, edition of *The Proceedings Against the Templars*. The assistance of others who helped in a wide variety of ways has also to be acknowledged. In particular, thanks are due to Samuel Winter for technical advice and for some of the photographs used; to Dr Christopher Harrison for historical advice, to librarians in the Local History section of Keele University Library, to the Parochial Church Council for permitting access to Keele Parish Church and its muniments, and to those local residents who, in the tradition of Rev. T.H. Brookes, sometime incumbent of this living, have been regaled with fragments of recently discovered information about the window whether they wished to hear it or not. I am particularly grateful to those who were not put off and have contributed to this publication, and those residents, of course, include my wife to whom this work is dedicated.

Chronology

1095	Pope Urban II preaches the FIRST CRUSADE at Clermont
1097	First Crusade arrives in Constantinople
1098	Capture of Antioch and Edessa (lost 1144)
1099	JERUSALEM captured
1128	Military Order of the KNIGHTS TEMPLAR licensed by pope
1147	SECOND CRUSADE, led by German Emperor, Conrad III, and French king, Louis VII
1158-63	Templar house at Keele founded
1169	Saladin occupies Cairo
1187	Saladin wins Battle of Hattin and then takes Jerusalem
1191	THIRD CRUSADE led by Philip II (Augustus), king of France and Richard I, king of England.

Acre recaptured by Richard

1204 FOURTH CRUSADE Constantinople captured

c.1216 Templar preceptory independent of its mother house established at Keele

1229 Emperor Frederick II's crusade - takes Jerusalem

1244 Turks re-capture Jerusalem

1249 First Crusade of Louis IX, king of France

Damietta (Egypt) captured by French king

1250 Louis IX and his crusader forces captured and imprisoned at Mansourah

1260 Mongols defeated by Mamluks; Baibars becomes Sultan in Egypt

1268 Baibars captures Antioch

1270 Second crusade of King Louis IX

St Louis dies at Tunis (25 August)

1271-2	Lord Edward's crusade
1272	Gregory X elected pope
1274	Gregory X summons The Council of Lyons to propose the renewal of crusading
1282	Thomas Totty claimed he had been admitted to the Templar Order at Keele
1287	Edward I renews his crusading vows
1288	Nicholas IV becomes pope
1290	Edward I petitions the pope to provide financial assistance to intending crusaders
1291	Acre lost after a two-month siege
1292	Provincial chapter of Canterbury archdiocese meets at the Temple in London, to push for a new crusade
	Edward I promises to take the cross and to set out on crusade in June 1293

Jacques de Molay elected to position of Grand Master of the Templar Order

1293 Jacques de Molay, arrives in England from Aragon to promote new crusade

Molay's itinerary in England is largely conjectural December. Meeting with Edward I in London

Was he at Keele on 24 June, Feast of St John the Baptist?

Said to have been at Garway in November

Was he at Keele on 15 August, Feast of the Assumption?

1294 Molay visits Eagle and Temple Bruer in January

1295 15 August: Thomas Totty received into the Templar Order at Keele

1307 Philip IV, king of France makes allegations of heresy against the Templars (September). And the pope issued orders for the arrest of all members of the Order (October- November). Many abscond from The Order

1308 Edward II confirmed the papal order

Officers of the sheriff of Staffordshire and Shropshire take Keele into royal hands

Ralph Tanet paid 4d per day as preceptor of Keele until late September 1309

1309 The pope appoints inquisitors to hear charges against the Templars in England, Scotland and Ireland

Templar brethren from Northern Province moved to prison in York or Lincoln

Thomas Totty held at Lincoln

Templar brethren from the Southern Province sent to The Tower of London

Ralph Tanet held in The Tower

1310	April: Thomas Totty interrogated at Lincoln
	12 May: 54 French Templars summarily burnt at the stake outside Paris
1311	25 June: Thomas Totty arrested and brought to trial in St Martin Vintry, London
1314	18 March - Paris: Jacques de Molay and a second Templar burnt at the stake
1322	Battle of Boroughbridge
	Keele treated as contrariant's land
1324	Knights Hospitaller take possession of Keele
1868-71	The parish church of St John the Baptist completely rebuilt by Ralph Sneyd of Keele Hall to the design of Thomas Lewis of Newcastle-under-Lyme

1

INTRODUCTION: THE TEMPLARS AT KEELE

The Knights Templar were the oldest of the military orders of chivalry. They were licensed as a new Order of knights in 1128. In this way formal recognition was given to the role that individual knights and others had been playing, providing protection to pilgrims and others then flocking in increasing numbers to the Holy Land on the heels of the success of the First Crusade in 1098. That had been an astoundingly successful enterprise but, by the early years of the twelfth century, it required organization and structure. The Templars were laymen, not monks or clerics, and had to be provided with a set of rules under which members could live. That was substantially the achievement of the great Cistercian monk, St Bernard of Clairvaux. However, because they were not ordained to the priesthood, the Templars had to always use the services of priests as chaplains to assist them.

Outside Europe a permanent military presence to support the new Kingdom of Jerusalem, to police pilgrims and travellers, and, aggressively, to act in defence of the roads leading to Jerusalem, became essential very quickly. The Templars were therefore installed in the Al Aqsa mosque next to the site of Solomon's Temple at the very heart of Jerusalem. Theirs was primarily a military role as Christ's policeman and because of their successful soldiering they found themselves looking after the large deposits of cash needed by crusaders in the field and on the journey east. Even in these early years the seeds of their downfall were being sown.

In the West, the Templars began to colonise the land with their settlements. Progress was slow initially. In England, their first houses were set up just ten years after the Order's foundation, at Dover, Shipley (Sussex) and the Old Temple in London[2]. About forty years later, at a date between 1158 and 1163 the Templars arrived

---

[2] The Templars settled first in a location at the junction of Chancery Lane and Holborn but moved to the new Temple, off Fleet Street, which became the headquarters of the English Order, in 1161.

in North Staffordshire, and by this time fourteen other Templar houses had been created across England. By the end of the thirteenth century not far short of sixty Templar foundations had been founded in these islands, all to raise money to pay for the Templars in the Holy Land.

[Fig.2: Famagusta, Cyprus - The Twin Churches: Knights Templar Church (right); Knights Hospitaller church (left).]

Although, in Europe, other military orders, appeared in the twelfth century devoted to crusading, in England, the only rivals to the Templars were the Knights Hospitaller. The Hospitallers emerged as a separate Order in the 1130s, and were regarded, at least initially, as having a distinctly different rationale. Like the Templars they too grew out of a disparate group of enthusiasts for the crusade. They offered care to the sick and infirm making their way to Jerusalem, acted as almoners, and recruited service in the crusading movement but, in many respects, they resembled their more military counterparts and, ultimately made it easy for unscrupulous political leaders to play one order off against the other. There was much scope for rivalry. Both main military orders depended on their ability to successfully raise income from their landed estates. Competition was fierce, and disputes were inevitable and often bitter.

In Staffordshire, however, this was not a major issue. Keele was the only house in the county of the two military orders operating in England. It was founded by Henry II, not long after his accession, and certainly before 1163, and was located in a part of the county where there was extensive uncleared, and largely uncolonized woodland. The name 'Keele' appears to derive from place name elements meaning 'a woodland clearing for cattle'. Keele was given to the Templar Order to reward it for loyally supporting King Henry II in Normandy during his quarrel with the French king. The initial royal grant was particularly generous as it included the entire Hundred of Pirehill which covered the whole of the north-western quarter of the county. In this way an estate was created which stretched from just north of Stafford to beyond Biddulph. The king, however, must have been astounded by his own generosity; it certainly looks as if he had miscalculated and had little idea of the extent of his grant for, shortly afterwards, he revoked it, leaving the Templars with a rump of their original endowment comprising; by 1163, lands in Newcastle-under-Lyme, Penkhull, Leycett and Keele, together worth a mere three and a quarter marks (£2 3s.4d.) according to the Pipe Roll of 1168/9. This had risen in value to eight marks a year (£5 6s.8d.) by 1185, an increase in value of the estate not far short of 200% in 17 years. The figures indicate that Keele was viable and of sufficient value for this new Templar estate to be organized administratively, eventually with its own preceptory. It was now of modest dimensions which were soon to be increased by gifts of often very small parcels of land from aspiring crusaders, recruits to the Order, pious benefactions and other sources of donation. In these matters, the Order was modestly successful in building up an estate centred on Keele across Staffordshire, Shropshire and Cheshire[3].

Within fifty years of its foundation a preceptory of the Templar Order was established on the hill at Keele and became the administrative hub of the Staffordshire Templar estate reaching into three counties. At its heart was the Templar chapel of the Virgin Mary, which was later re-dedicated to St John the Baptist by the Hospitallers in the third decade of the fourteenth century. From the twelfth to the fourteenth centuries the Order had the capacity to attract money and members to its ranks. It also attracted privilege. Because the Templars were an exempt order, answerable directly to the pope and none other they were not subject to the authority of the local bishop at

[3] R. Studd, 'A Templar Colony in North Staffordshire: Keele before the Sneyds', in Essays on the History of Keele, ed, C. J. Harrison (1986), 6-10.

Lichfield, or to his archdeacon or to any of his officers. Privileges of this kind covered not just the Templar brethren but all the Order's tenants and servants and were the cause of considerable jealousy from the members of established religious orders. The Templars were answerable only to the pope himself and his legates. This resulted in a degree of personal freedom, not experienced by non-exempt religious elsewhere and unsurprisingly, other orders were resentful of this and challenged it from time to time making it essential that both military orders should be especially vigilant in guarding their unusual privilege.

Several European rulers attempted to bypass what they regarded as an obstacle to their ability to govern their own territory unimpeded, as this matter became an issue for many. In 1284, for instance, Pope Martin IV instructed the king of Cyprus to desist from his attempts to tax the Templars in the island and to stop seizing their property when they failed to pay up. Boniface VIII repeated the order in 1295 and indicated that he regarded their privileged status as compensation for the scale of past losses endured by the Order in supporting the crusades and in defending Christians against the forces of Islam. Even in Keele this issue mattered and had particular relevance after the demise of the Templars, as we shall see.

As an ecclesiastical peculiar, Keele was not served by a parish priest but by the Templar's chaplains and, after 1314, because the Knights Hospitaller were also exempt, by their chaplains. A parish guild to coordinate the religious life of the parish, assisted by two parish reeves, had come into existence at Keele by 1354, but its dedication, to the Blessed Virgin Mary, strongly suggests that it began when the Templars held sway at Keele. By 1467 each householder in the parish was being charged fourpence a year to meet the costs of the chaplain. Keele was still not organized as a parish at this point but retained its peculiar status until the end of the medieval period. A parish was not organized at Keele until after the Sneyds acquired the manorial title and there is evidence to suggest that it probably did not happen until late in the seventeenth century, when the Sneyds had established a permanent presence here. Indeed, from the time of the arrival of the Sneyds in

North Staffordshire, Keele was treated as an adjunct of the parish of Wolstanton, which the Sneyds had also acquired in the reign of Henry VIII.

Under the Templars, Keele had become the central unit of a north Staffordshire group of the Order's holdings which was initially run as a dependency of the preceptory at Temple Dinsley in Hertfordshire. Donations to the Templars at Keele continued to be made throughout the course of the twelfth and thirteenth centuries and included several estates in Shropshire, while the Audleys, as lords of neighbouring Heighley Castle, gave them lands in Balterley and Nantwich, and a small estate at Onneley and Madeley. The Keele Templar estate grew in importance and value and, in this way, was able to escape from its initial dependence on Temple Dinsley, although a link between the two houses seems to have been maintained, for Ralph Tanet, the only Templar brother resident at Keele, when members of the Order were arrested in 1308, had been admitted to the Templars at

Dinsley in 1297. However, shortly after 1216 Keele became an independent Templar preceptory[4].

In theory, each preceptory had an officer of the order, called a preceptor, in charge who was provided with his own separate residence standing apart from the farm which was at the centre of the preceptory complex, as can still be seen at Garway (Herefordshire), but also at Keele. The preceptors were often knights, men of military standing answerable to the Grand Master of the Order and with a duty to attend its provincial chapter meetings. It was not always the case, however; evidence from the Templars' trial in 1311 suggests that long before the early fourteenth century knights were a comparative rarity in the Order. The preceptor of Ewell in Surrey, for example, called himself Ralph of Maldon, but before the provincial council of Canterbury in 1311, he was styled Ralph the carpenter of Maldon, almost certainly reflecting the reality of his social status. The qualifications for knighthood that the Order had depended on in the twelfth century could no

---

[4] R. Studd, 'A Templar Colony in North Staffordshire: Keele before the Sneyds', *Essays on the History of Keele. ed. C. Harrison (1986),* 6-8.

longer be met with facility in the thirteenth. Even if they were born legitimate, few among the senior ranks

[Fig.3: Garway (Herefordshire) from the west. Note the freestanding fortified tower and church (centre & left) and the preceptor's house (rt.). The relationship of the church to the preceptor's house is similar to the arrangement at Keele.]

of the Templars by this date were of knightly stock or had the income to support that status. At Keele, at its dissolution in 1307, there was no knight present on the manorial estate. Its administration was, therefore, entrusted to Ralph Tanet, a sergeant of the order, who was of lower rank than a knight, and who, at one point in the record, is, even so, but unusually, styled 'deputy preceptor'[5].

It was the sergeants who were in day to day charge of what were, in effect, extended farms whose purpose was to raise cash not just to support local Templar requirements but also to produce a surplus which could be used to contribute to Templar effort throughout Europe and overseas. The work of running these farmsteads quite often fell to the sergeants. 'The non-military sergeants or serving Brothers', as Professor Nicholson has pointed out, 'did manual work, such as carpentry, looking after animals, acting as smiths or stone masons'[6]. The whole rationale of the Templars was to raise cash to support the work of The Temple in Jerusalem, to provide a military presence in the Holy Land, and through engagement in various agricultural

---

[5] In his account of the manor of Keele, Roger Trumwyne, a former sheriff of Staffordshire and Shropshire refers to an indenture, dated January 1308, made in the presence of the knight, William de Stafford and, brother Ralph de Tanet, *custos* of the house at Keele, and, later in the same account records Ralph was paid wages as preceptor of Keele (P.R.O., E358/20 m.5d.).

[6] Helen Nicholson, *The Knights Templar: A brief History of the warrior Order* (2010), 137.

and related activities to assist those, pilgrims and others, who made the perilous journey to the Middle East. The rare, probably unique, image of sergeants in the Keele window illustrates very precisely the kind of work they undertook. Here they are stonemasons.

As a sergeant, rather than as 'deputy preceptor', Ralph Tanet is likely to have had a broad range of primarily agricultural duties overseeing the running of the Keele estate. When the preceptor of Keele abandoned his post, Ralph*, custos* (warden) of Keele had the necessary competence to step in and the manorial accounts for the period, which survive in part, indicate that the Keele estate was satisfactorily managed at this time[7]. Ralph Tanet, who appears to have been a relatively new recruit to the Order with less than ten years of service, seems to have been largely compliant and certainly did not occasion the level of hostility meted out to others by the inquisitors in 1311.

---

[7] The accounts which are deliberately not discussed here, may be found at The National Archives (Kew), E358/18; E358/19 and E358/20. An edition is currently available on Professor Nicholson's website.

At the heart of each preceptory stood the Templar's chapel which record evidence suggests was built at Keele in the mid-thirteenth century. A striking image of the Templar chapel in its landscape setting of c. 1850 survives in the William Salt Library at Stafford (See Fig. 9b). This shows a rectangular crenelated structure with three window openings and a door on its northern elevation with an attached square tower at its west end. The church is depicted standing some metres apart from the vicarage which served originally as the preceptor's house in a relationship which replicates that at the Templar preceptory at Garway in Herefordshire and indicates a common element in the planning of Templar houses. Other surviving images of the church confirm its medieval date and show that the chapel stood throughout the later medieval and early modern period largely untouched. A water colour of its interior, done in about 1860, indicates the presence of thirteenth-century window tracery openings in the south wall. Substantial internal remodelling, rather than a reconstruction, took place in the last decade of the eighteenth century when its fine seventeenth-century wooden screen was relocated, and a new setting created for its marble font. Although an account of the church in the 1811 number of *Gentleman's Magazine* is laced with heraldic records of every memorial, and has a full description of Barbara Sneyd's embroidered fitments for the church, there is unfortunately no mention of the church's glass. However, presiding over a mere chapel, however, much modernized in the eighteenth century, was not to the taste of a patron with aspirations to gentility and a strongly competitive attitude towards his Staffordshire neighbours.

The medieval structure was entirely swept away when the present parish church of St John the Baptist at Keele was built by Ralph Sneyd between 1868 and 1871. Even its tower was taken down and relocated from the west end to the south west corner of the rebuilt church. No trace of the medieval church remained above ground level; the only indication of its Templar origin is to be found in the window glass re-located in the choir vestry.

[Fig.4: Keele - Masons building the new Jerusalem: note their ruffs and flat caps, and the tools of their trade. This is probably a unique image of Templar serving brothers.]

The Templar chapel which, from surviving images of parts of the building, appears to have been built in the early thirteenth century, stood throughout the early modern period, as evidenced by a watercolour of the church interior, done in 1860, showing thirteenth-century window tracery openings in the north wall[8]. Substantial internal remodelling, rather than a reconstruction, took place in the last decade of the eighteenth century when its fine seventeenth-century wooden screen was relocated, and a new setting created for its marble font.[9] Although the account in the 1811 number of *Gentleman's Magazine* is laced with heraldic records of every memorial, and has a full description of Barbara Sneyd's embroidered fitments for the church, there is, unfortunately no mention of the church's glass. Presiding over a mere chapel, however much modernized in the previous century, was not to the taste of a patron with aspirations to

[8] Lichfield Cathedral Library. Moore and Hinckes drawings, 21 no.8 (illustrated in *VCH, Staffordshire*, XI (2013).

[9] *The Gentleman's Magazine*, LXXXI (2) (1811), 306-8 & illustrated with comment in *VCH, Staffordshire,* XI, 16,18.

gentility and a strongly competitive attitude towards his Staffordshire neighbours.

The present parish church of St John the Baptist at Keele was built for Ralph Sneyd between 1868 and 1871.The medieval structure was completely taken down and its tower removed. No trace of the medieval

[Fig.5: Charlotte Sneyd's pen and wash drawing of houses in 1820s Keele include a faint image of the church, with a tower (top rt.) Keele University Archives: Sneyd Collection.]

church remained above ground; the only indication of its Templar origin is to be found in the window glass relocated in the choir vestry. Although the Templar's foundation documents were the brainchild of the great Cistercian monk, Bernard of Clairvaux, and their houses were much less imposing, and less formally structured than their Cistercian exemplars, some of the unfussiness and the same repetitive economy of design of the monastic order can be detected in Templar houses too. The footprint of Keele's Templar church is, however, known from muniments kept in the church.

They reveal that it was rectangular in form, with a tower at its south-west corner. It lay directly underneath the nave of the present building and almost entirely within it. It was conceived as a plain, simple structure, and, at Keele, did not have any element of the favoured Templar round church form known to have been present in at least six other Templar churches in England such as at Dover, Temple Bruer and Garway. It is possible that it may have had an internal apse in the manner of some Templar buildings, such as at Garway, and was rather like the church that still stands at Famagusta in Cyprus which was the principal church of the Templar Order in the island. This has a single lancet shaped light for glazing for an east window in the centre of the apse, and, it is suspected, replicates the arrangement at Keele.

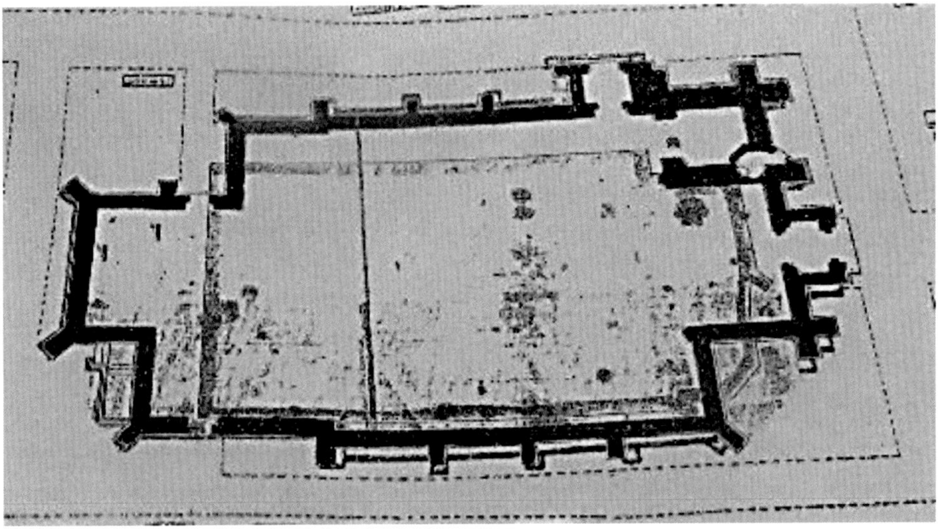

[Fig.6: Plan of St John the Baptist, Parish Church. Keele, built 1868-70, with the outline of the location of a smaller medieval Templar church lying almost entirely within the Victorian church. The Templar chapel had a square end in the Burgundian style. There is no evidence here of a circular church found in a handful of English Templar houses elsewhere. The footings of a tower are indicated at the SW corner of the medieval church (bottom right of the plan). (copyright St John's, Keele, PCC)]

[Fig.7: Famagusta Templar church, apse with lancet window.]

However, it is not possible to be certain that this was how the window opening(s) were ordered here since, for instance, the Templar church at Garway, has triple openings for lights. Unfortunately, any drawings that Clayton and Bell made of Keele, which could resolve this issue, were lost in the Blitz.

[Fig.8: Garway (Herefordshire): Templar church. Note the triple opening for lights in the chancel which is rectangular in form. The church was remodelled by the Knights Hospitaller after 1312 to create a rectangular nave. The only evidence of the Templar's circular church can be seen here in the short length of circular masonry - here painted cream - immediately above the hymn board. Footings of the church exposed outside the north side of the nave provide other evidence of its circular form.]

As we see it today, St John's church is a good example of a nineteenth-century estate church built by, and to the glory of, its local squire's family. That is what Ralph Sneyd intended. He spent the bulk of his income from the local coal and iron industries on building this Grade II* listed structure between 1868 and 1871 to replace its smaller medieval predecessor which, in Sneyd's time, was regarded as too humble and unsuitable for the place of worship of a country squire with a strong opinion of his own social worth[10]. Sneyd's building, to a design by his patron's favoured local Staffordshire architect, Thomas Lewis of Newcastle-under-Lyme, warrants its listing for its unchanged nineteenth century interior and for the quality of its Clayton and Bell, mainly geometric, stained glass windows,

---

10 The Sneyd family has an unfortunate record for the destruction of medieval buildings. Early in the 17th century, at a time when it was leased by a member of the family from the Duchy of Lancaster, what remained of the castle buildings at Newcastle-under-Lyme were demolished, including 'one great toure' (R.A. Brown, H.M. Colvin & A.J. Taylor, *The History of the King's Works*, ii (1963), 749).

including grisaille work in its clerestory, with a yellow stain imitating medieval glass.

[Fig.9a: Keele, St John the Baptist, parish church, 1868-70 stands on the site of the Templar church. Note its elevated position as favoured by the Knights Templar. The preceptory occupied land in the foreground and across the new walled access road (centre) created by Andrew Thompson in the 1840s, to the right of the graveyard.]

The church of St John the Baptist, Keele, was built as a single architectural scheme over three years. It is, therefore, a thoroughly typical example of a Victorian Anglican squire's conceit, providing a retrospective setting for his ancestors' memorials, re-erected and re-hung on the walls of his new church, which was furnished to emphasise the squire's paternalistic interest in his parishioners. Here, especially narrow seating at the rear of the church for the children of the congregation and numbered seats for the adults in the body of the church demonstrate the gulf between the lord and his tenants in this closed social community. All was set off by fine Minton tiles on the chancel floor, Victorian Gothic figurative corbels in the nave, and a full set of stained glass windows in the clerestory, nave aisles, chancel, lady chapel and east end, while the east end of the church was extended to provide sufficient space for a family vault. A few of the windows have figurative designs typical of the period but the majority, and those of by far the highest quality, are Clayton and Bell's windows with complex geometrical patterns. Each is subtly different, demonstrating the finest in their repertoire; they have consequently been selected for listing.

There is considerable extant additional evidence, archaeological and otherwise on the present site and in its vicinity to demonstrate the existence of a Templar house at Keele. To begin with, the site of the preceptory here is on a hill which rises over 600 feet above sea level which, to this day, is in a commanding position in its landscape, with the parish church at its highest point. In this respect, it conforms with what we know of the siting of many other Templar foundations in England, such as at Dover, Garway (Herefordshire), or Temple Newsam (Yorkshire) and elsewhere in Europe such as Peniscola (Valencia), Miravet (Catalonia) or La Couvertoirade (Aveyron). These were all conscious attempts, as appropriate in each situation, to imitate the location of The Temple Mount in Jerusalem where, after 1108, within the Al Aqsa Mosque, the Templars set up their headquarters in the Holy Land.

At Keele, the former preceptor's house, later the rectory, a substantial property with medieval cellars and an eighteenth-century brick-casing, lies just to the north-west of the parish church. An ancient hollow way leading to the preceptory ran through the site and is now clearly visible on its eastern boundary.

[Fig.9b: Keele church and parsonage 19th century – by kind permission of the William Salt Library.]

[Fig.10: Keele, Preceptor's House. The 18th century cased structure has medieval cellars.]

It was once part of a track which zig-zagged through the landscape from Newcastle-under-Lyme in the east towards Shropshire across the high land which separates Keele from Madeley to the west, and now provides a shared entrance to the former preceptor's house and the parish church.

[Fig.11: Keele - the medieval hollow way, which follows the walled perimeter of the preceptory (right), leads to the preceptor's house and the church. A glimpse can be had in the distance of the 19th century new road (A525) created to improve access to Keele.]

Evidence of unexcavated earlier structures, lie on either side of Keele Road. These are unattributed but, if comparison is made with other Templar houses such as Garway or Temple Balsall, they presumably contain the imprint of a dovecote, brewhouse, buttery, dairy and other structures associated with farming and agriculture which are not specifically located at Keele, although they do occur in the extant Templar accounts for Keele. The building named Old Hall at Temple Balsall was excavated in the 1970s was found to enclose a multi-purpose, thirteenth century, open hall[11].

[Fig.12: The Old Hall, Temple Balsall. The 13th century Templar hall was discovered within the single storey cased element (rt.); the church (far rt.), and the two- storey wing (left) were the work of the Hospitallers and date from the 14th century.]

---

[11] E. Gooder, *Temple Balsall: The Warwickshire Preceptory of the Templars and their fate* (1995), 64-80.

The Old Hall at Keele is marked on nineteenth century maps just below the church. It was situated right across the line of the Keele Road and presumably served an identical purpose to its Warwickshire counterpart. The site of the Keele preceptory farm buildings has been distorted by the creation of a nineteenth-century 'bypass' (the former A525) driven through the settlement by Andrew Thompson, a distinguished inspector to the Inclosure Commissioners, who was also Ralph Sneyd's Agent and lived in Keele at The Hawthorns. Thompson was an agricultural reformer at the forefront of a movement in the 1840s to provide modern farms and acceptable housing for farm workers. Keele's farms and its cottages are his legacy as is the redesign of the entire settlement, intended to facilitate easier access to the village and beyond[12]. Beneath Thompson's changes, however, the Templar preceptory has also left its mark. Small finds from field walking associated with the preceptory have turned up from time to time, such as a fragment of a medieval

[12] *The Staffordshire Reports of Andrew Thompson to the Inclosure Commissioners, 1858-68 ...*, ed A.D.M. Phillips (Staffordshire Record Society, 1996).

bell, equestrian fittings, and pre-Reformation silver coins, while ashlar blocks and quarried pieces of masonry may be found in walls and gardens in the vicinity re-used as hardcore, or, decoratively in rockeries.

Fig.13(a-c). Pieces of sandstone masonry may be found in village gardens and retaining walls and provide evidence of the presence of the Templar preceptory at Keele.

However, most significantly within the parish church, there survive substantial fragments of medieval window glass of considerable interest. The window from which these remain is the focus of this monograph.

What is remarkable is that the glass is almost wholly unrecorded. In 1961 Peter Newton wrote a distinguished thesis on 'Schools of Glass Painting in the Midlands, 1275-1450'[13], surveying all the extant medieval glass in eight counties, including Staffordshire, but he simply missed it. The window is not noticed in the listing of painted and stained glass in the *Corpus Vitrearum* and gets short shrift from those who gave the parish church its Grade II* listing. It merits no mention in any standard guidebook. From 1954 to 1972 the vicar of Keele was Rev. T. H. Brookes. He was an enquiring man and was the only person at the time to suggest that the window deserved more considered scrutiny than it had received up to that

[13] Peter A. Newton, 'Schools of Glass Painting in the Midlands, 1275-1430', London University, PhD thesis 1961.

point. In a pamphlet he produced in 1970 to celebrate the centenary of Keele's Parish church, he wrote,

> 'It is a cause for great thankfulness, that, when the present Church was erected, the thread of continuity with previous Churches was preserved. For first of all, there is, in the Choir Vestry, a precious stained-glass window of the fourteenth century. I am vastly intrigued by this window, for it depicts a small Church which may well be the Chapel of the Blessed Virgin Mary...'[14]

Brookes' hunch was well informed, although he failed in his account to comment on the antiquity of the rectory in which he lived. The dating he suggests is debatable, the glass is mainly painted rather than stained and the church depicted in the window was not at all small. The connection with the Virgin Mary is absolutely accurate, however, and securely based. Like all Templar foundations, that at Keele was dedicated to the Virgin Mary, with her principal festival, the Feast of

---

[14] T.H. Brookes, (1970), 12.

the Assumption (15 August), celebrated here. As we shall discover the window is dedicated to the Virgin but is also much more, for, not only does it present strong evidence of the presence of the Knights Templar at Keele but also relates directly to papal attempts to revitalise the crusading efforts of all western Europeans in the thirteenth century.

2

Crusading in the thirteenth century: the Templar window in context

The enthusiasm for crusading in the early thirteenth century, which the Templars embodied, was curbed by military failure. Political rivalry amongst the crusaders and the two disastrous crusades of St Louis - the French king, Louis IX - had blunted its appeal. His first crusade culminated in the king's capture at Mansourah in Egypt in 1250, and the latter ended with in his death from disease before Tunis in 1270.

For its participants crusading became a particularly perilous enterprise after 1250, following the seizure of power in Egypt and Syria by the forces of Islam, and the creation of a Mamluk sultanate. It also became much more personally expensive for any setting out to defend the Holy Places in this century. Crusades could be called by the pope alone but, within Christendom, the business of drumming up enthusiasm for crusading fell to the two principal military orders of Knights

Templar and Hospitaller. Persuading the leaders of Europe to participate was one of the primary duties of these Orders and presented particular problems by the thirteenth century for all. It had been easy to tap general enthusiasm for crusading after the success of the First Crusade, and there was, by and large, undiminished support for crusading until about 1200, but after that, it was necessary for crusading protagonists to resort to propaganda to raise funds and gather popular support.

Persuading the ordinary folk of Europe to engage in the crusading ideal to the extent that they had done in the previous century was also a difficult call which is addressed by the surviving panel of fragments of medieval painted glass in St John's Parish Church, Keele. This is, as we shall see, a piece of unrestrained political propaganda for crusading. By these means crusading was encouraged and given an important local dimension.

[Fig.14: The glass fragments in the lower part of the window comprise elements representing The Assumption of the Virgin. Here we have an image of the crowned Virgin as 'Queen of Heaven', rocks from which the Virgin ascended, clouds through which she rose, blue sky and the sun. The buildings depicted are of the city of Jerusalem being rebuilt. The lions' heads and ballflowers symbolise Christ the king and the Virgin Mary.]

Englishmen were especially prominent crusaders and frequently followed the example set, in taking the cross, by a number of English kings, and their children. Richard I, John, Henry III, his brother, Richard of Cornwall, and his son, the Lord Edward, the future

Edward I were all enthusiastic supporters even when they were not crusaders themselves. Undertaking a crusade was a very costly venture but, until the last decade of the thirteenth century, could count on royal support, which in turn encouraged popular and magnate enthusiasm. As a consequence, there was a receptive audience for crusading propaganda in thirteenth-century England.

The crusading enterprises of The Lord Edward are particularly pertinent in the context of this study. Edward joined his brother-in-law, Louis IX of France, in 1270, on his second crusade to the Holy Land, sailing from Aigues Mortes, on the Mediterranean coast, on 2 July 1270 for Sardinia, as a first stage in the journey. Two weeks later the crusaders were outside Tunis, whose emir, King Louis had learned, intended to convert. There the crusade halted as the heat took its toll; many were struck down by sickness, and King Louis died on 25 August. The remnant of the crusaders retreated to Sicily before dispersing, but Edward continued with his company of crusaders to the Holy Land. The decision to carry on with St Louis' crusade after the French king's death brought Edward great kudos. He was now the unquestioned champion of Christendom.

Although Edward's crusade achieved little militarily, we know that while crusading between April 1271 and September 1272, he was at Acre and Caesarea, as well as, the birthplace of St George, at Lydda. At the fortress of Qaqun he negotiated a lengthy truce with the Mamluk leader, Baibars. More importantly, Edward made personal contacts with the leading exponents of crusading of his day. These included Otto de Grandison, who served the Templars at Acre until its fall and would later become Edward's personal representative first, in the Channel Islands, and later as his Lieutenant in Aquitaine. In 1272, he was named with others, by the Lord Edward as an executor with power to administer all his lands, to protect his children and to oversee the succession to the kingdom should his father, Henry III, die. In the event, it was Edward who nearly died after an assassin attempted to kill him on 17 June that year. Arrangements to safeguard the succession were in the meantime, made on the very next day in the presence of the most important witnesses then in Acre. These included Hugh Revel, the master of the Hospital and Thomas Berard, master of the Temple at Acre, but also, and, chief among them, Teobaldo Visconti, Archdeacon of Liège, who was elected to the papal throne as Gregory X with Edward in Sicily during their return journey to the west. All these events demonstrated Edward's pivotal role as the leader of the crusade and marked him out as the preferred leader of any future crusade, and as the most qualified European statesman, who would need to be consulted before any further crusade could be launched.

But it was the pope, Gregory X, Edward's companion and co-crusader, who seized the initiative by summoning the Council of Lyons (1274) to discuss the renewal of crusades to the east and the recovery of the Holy Land. Preaching a new crusade at the end of the Council meeting in July 1274, the pope succeeded in putting crusading back on the political agenda of western Europeans. While Gregory X lived there was optimism that the crusades could be re-launched but the prospect was undercut by inadequate consideration of the practical issues which needed to be taken into account. This resulted, in subsequent years, in a series of tracts, many sceptical, on how the recovery of the Holy Places might be accomplished; little was achieved to advance the likelihood of the progress of such a venture. Although the pope succeeded, in part, in raising cash for a renewed crusading effort, weak and non-existent papal leadership after Gregory X's death in 1276, and the ambitions of Charles of Anjou to create a Mediterranean empire for himself, diverted attention from crusading.

The idea of mounting a full crusade for the recovery of the Holy Places was not lost in these years but had no chance of securing the political direction required. When Edward I renewed his crusading vows in 1287 he found himself unable to deliver due to his wars in Wales and Scotland and his political disagreements with the French kings, Philip III and Philip IV. Commercial rivalry between the Venetians and the Genoese often erupted into open conflict and did so at this point. It also diverted attention from Islamic achievements in the east. Nor did the Military Orders, especially The Templars, provide the kind of leadership required and, being mainly recruited from among the ranks of the lesser nobility, they lacked the essential political and military clout needed. The Templars were often accused by contemporary chroniclers, such as Matthew Paris, and others, of self-interest and lack of commitment to the common purpose of crusading[15]. Their critics were right. Not surprisingly, Mamluk advances continued unchecked in this period. Both Latakia (1287) and Tripoli (1290) fell to Islamic forces.

Pope Nicholas IV, responded by stepping up demands on Europe's secular leaders to organize a new crusade. In 1288 Nicholas issued an instruction to all Christians either to donate directly to the crusade or to commit publicly to participate in it. The Keele window would seem to be a positive response to the pope's call for action. It expresses visually a sermon designed to encourage prayers, special devotion and other religious activities in support of crusaders and crusading. It also aimed to bolster lay devotion by providing an image

[15] E. Burman, *The Templars, Knights of God* (1986), 141-5.

that local people could understand in the form of a devotional representation of the Virgin in the most vivid format available at the time - brilliant stained and painted glass - in juxtaposition with images of the new Jerusalem being built in response to the sanctioning of a new crusade. To the Templars of Keele and local people the message was clear and could be read in the glazing of their window. Saving Jerusalem and the Holy Places from the Infidel was their primary duty as Christians; paying for it was equally essential.

In 1290 Edward I successfully petitioned the pope, as its prospective leader, to grant financial assistance for the proposed new crusade, which was to be paid by all lords not intending to join the venture. But by this date the position of the crusader territories in the east was all but irretrievable, and their fate was finally sealed by the fall of Acre, after a siege lasting from early April to mid-May 1291. Acre was the largest city in the Latin Kingdom of Jerusalem and the headquarters in the east of both the Templars and Hospitallers. Its loss was catastrophic; the slaughter was considerable. The Templars present at the siege were massacred almost to a man; few escaped to Cyprus. Edward I's plans to resume crusading were put on hold.

Nicholas IV, who had become pope in 1288, was, however, still determined to promote a general crusade and had already renewed his call for action a month before the disaster at Acre[16]. Nicholas demonstrated his willingness to put whatever pressure might be needed to ensure that the leaders of Europe would take his crusading message seriously and to make the recovery of the lost Holy Places their priority. Like his predecessor, Gregory X, the pope responded swiftly to events, first, by attempting to organize a crusade to the small Christian kingdom of Armenia to relieve Mamluk attacks there and, second, by trying to re-invigorate crusading to the Holy Land, directed, especially, to the recovery of Jerusalem.

To this end Nicholas IV needed to secure the active assistance of the west. In England, this amounted to ordering the re-issue of his earlier papal bulls instructing the archbishops and all bishops to preach

---

[16] Simon Lloyd, *English Society and the Crusade 1236-1307* (1988), 44-6.

the Cross throughout the kingdom, and also seeking help in how, practically, the crusading message could be conveyed. As a result, a provincial chapter of the English Church was summoned to meet at The Temple in London on 13 February 1292 putting Templar efforts at the forefront of the push for a new crusade. The 'business of the Holy Land', as thirteenth-century shorthand had it, embraced the whole of Christendom; none were exempt[17].

This was a significant moment in the history of crusading in the thirteenth century; it was the point at which protagonists of crusading could have achieved their goal of reviving crusading. Several events came together to make this more likely than before. In Cyprus a new Grand Master of the Templar Order emerged by a process which has never been fully explained. Jacques de Molay very quickly made his mark as a thoroughly dynamic leader addressing, with the pope, the threats made to Armenia at the outset of his rule, even before he is first styled Grand Master of the Order in the record, in April 1292. Then, probably

---

17 F.M. Powicke, *The Thirteenth Century, 1216-1307* (1962), 80-83.

at the direction of Pope Nicholas, who viewed de Molay as his champion, the Grand Master's attention was directed to western Europe. In May 1293 he sailed from Cyprus for Provence where he intended to attend a General Chapter of his order at Montpellier. Historians have debated whether he also went to Aragon to enlist the support of its king, James II. The evidence of the Keele window, with its reference to Aragon suggests not only that it was possible but that it was most probable, and that this was the context in which the window, most likely, was commissioned and created.

Papal propaganda promoting a new crusade had clearly worked for, in spite of Nicholas IV's untimely death in April 1292, new energy seems to have been put into the crusading ideal; there was every chance that a new crusade could be launched. In England, too, crusading propaganda seems to have had some success for here there appears to have been real enthusiasm for it, with promises made of financial aid to crusaders who were prepared to set off. Some money was advanced and Edward I, at last, named the date of his departure for the east as 24 June 1293.

Early in 1292 all had seemed set fair for the crusade to take place led by an enthusiastic monarch, and in a general climate of positive support for the venture. However, events again intervened to halt Edward's preparations. The unresolved issue of the Scottish succession dragged on, preventing the king from leaving the kingdom while the vacancy on the papal throne following Pope Nicholas's death lasted for a further two years, until 1294, and was not resolved by the election of the unsuitable Celestine V to the papacy. The pro-crusading camp was left leaderless at a critical time. There can be no doubt that the English king remained supportive of the proposals to resume crusading at this time, and he readily met with the newly elected Grand Master when he arrived in England in 1293, determined to take up Nicholas IV's crusading cause. That this was the year that de Molay's window, with its striking crusade propaganda imagery, arrived in Keele demonstrates the interconnection of these events. The message of the window was intended to proselytize for crusading.

After the fall of Acre, the Knights Templar had to move their headquarters to Cyprus and it was from there, by way of Aragon, that Jacques de Molay, the new Templar Grand Master, travelled to England in 1293 in expectation of royal support for the several causes he was espousing at this time. These included resisting attempts by the established religious orders to compel a union of the main military orders, the Templars and Hospitallers, re-establishing a Templar presence in the Holy Land; and, of course, reviving the idea of a universal crusade. The Templars had been particularly privileged by their location in Jerusalem in the Al Aqsa Mosque within Solomon's Temple, at the very centre of the crusader Kingdom of Jerusalem; its loss in 1187 was a hammer blow to the crusaders which was somewhat offset by the subsequent capture of Acre by Richard I so that it remained in crusader hands for the next century. The fall of Acre in 1291 was therefore catastrophic. With no Holy Places to defend in Asia Minor, the rationale for crusading all but vanished. The Templars were blamed by many for the disaster. Psychologically and personally, the loss of Acre affected each of them. Many Templars, including de Molay's predecessor as Grand Master of the entire Order, had died there in battle. Traumatized and severely depleted in numbers, their withdrawal to Cyprus appeared to spell the end of influence for the Templar Order and, but for the personality and persistence of the man newly elected to the office of Grand Master of the Templar Order in 1292, that might have been the case.

The events of 1291 had severely damaged their credibility as an Order; they had lost face and now conceived themselves as having an overwhelming obligation to recover their lost territory in the Holy Land. Taking the Holy Places back into Christian hands and rebuilding the Holy City of Jerusalem became the central objective of a projected revival of the crusade. To achieve this, the popular support of the whole of Christendom was needed, for its members would be required to assist such a venture with money and manpower. A political leader able to command authority within Christendom who was also capable of leading troops in the field was also essential. That is why Jacques de Molay, Grand Master of the entire Templar Order, and leading propagandist for the

Templar cause, was despatched to England on his first European venture to the west to persuade the king of England of his responsibility as a Christian king, to take up the banner of crusading that he had last grasped twenty years previously.

[Fig. 15: Famagusta: Templar church - with cross patée of exemption used to designate Templar property. The Templars were an exempt order not subject to the authority of the local bishop and his officers. Crosses like this were set up wherever Templar estates needed to be distinguished from those that were subject to episcopal jurisdiction. The perimeter of the Templar estate at Keele would have been marked by crosses of this type, though, as yet none has been found.]

Because of his crusading credentials and reputation as a political and military figure, Edward I was the obvious choice to lead the proposed crusade – if only the English king could be persuaded to overcome his reluctance to take the cross. This was why the king met with the Grand Master in London on 8 December 1293.

There is also another possible reason why de Molay sought out Edward I, for it is intriguing to observe that Edward and de Molay may have met in Acre when they were both there in 1272. Inferences from their mutual behaviour in December 1293 is that they were longstanding friends. Unfortunately, there is no evidence to show that they had met in 1272. However, they shared a common experience and, in 1293, found a common purpose in a new crusading enterprise. Records show that they discussed outstanding shared issues concerning the operation of the Templar Order in England and it is also made clear that de Molay had previously visited other locations within the kingdom before he met the king. We learn, for instance, that the Grand Master had already been to the Templar preceptory at Cressing in Essex, probably the wealthiest Templar house in England, as part of a general tour of English Templar houses designed to encourage support for the proposed crusade.

The Grand Master was in England to hold chapter meetings of his Order which is a clear indication of its itinerant nature. But the precise route he followed, and its dating, is conjectural for the most part. We know only that his purpose was to promote the proposed crusade and that he was certainly at Garway (Herefordshire) in late November 1293. That much was part of the testimony of the Templar chaplain, John de Stoke, given at his trial in July 1311, when he is said to have been interrogated by the Grand Master in person. Subsequently, the Grand Master is known to have visited Eagle and Temple Bruer, two Lincolnshire houses, where he was in January 1294. But where else did he go? Unfortunately, the testimony of other Templar brethren is either deliberately silent on this matter, or else this part of the testimony of the brethren was suppressed and edited out by the clerks of the Inquisition. Hints that Temple Balsall (Warwickshire), among others, was visited are insufficiently explicit but, as we shall see, seems highly likely to have occurred. There is a much clearer, but rather different form of indication that Jacques de Molay did visit Keele, but it does not derive directly from the testimony given at the trial of the Templars. The clerks of the Inquisition, responsible for the surviving record were far too careful in controlling the evidence, excising issues that might be seen to be favourable to the Templars. In the absence of firm dates in the record, we need to turn detective. What we do know, and what we can piece together, suggests that certain dates for de Molay's presence in Keele, appear more probable than others, and will be discussed later. The principal evidence for his visit comes from a careful reading of the contents of the Templar window itself with its representation of the celebration of the Feast of the Assumption of the Virgin at its centre.

The Virgin Mary was the patron of the Order of Knights Templar, so that all Templar churches throughout Christendom were dedicated to her. Here the Virgin, as the single saint depicted in the window would have been placed in the centre of the composition directly beneath and protected by the characteristic later thirteenth-century crocketed canopy depicted at the centre of Clayton and Bell's reconstruction.

3

Reading the Templar Window

When the Templar chapel at Keele was taken down in 1868, the surviving fragments of medieval glass were collected together by Clayton and Bell and set up in a vestry area at the south west corner of the rebuilt parish church. Their work elsewhere, for example at Hessett in Suffolk, suggests they were careful to maintain the integrity of what they found, and so it seems to have been at Keele, such that it is still possible to discern content and meaning from the extant fragments of medieval glass.

Unfortunately, today the medieval window is somewhat obscured by incongruous 'improvements' done in the 1970s, including the insertion of toilet facilities and, although this has not caused damage to the window itself, it is a frustrating obstacle to an unimpeded appreciation of the window's glass.

The window was transferred from the east end of the original medieval church to the choir vestry after 1868. It is an ogee headed opening 113.5 cm. tall by 61 cm. wide with a pair of flanking mouchettes, each 27cm. in length. The lower register of the window is divided by a horizontal glazing bar which separates the coloured from the plain glass in the lower register. The upper sections including the mouchettes are filled with stained and painted glass with some plain nineteenth-century white glass demarking the shoulders and the ogee head. The upper registers contain more than sixty frames of separately leaded glass assembled in what at first glance appears to be a rather random fashion which, on the one hand is indicative of the scale of the loss of the medieval glass, but also seems to denote the approximate position in the general scheme of each frame in the original order. Clayton and Bell's glaziers appear to have taken considerable care to place each surviving fragment of window glass as close to where it may have been located in the original scheme. That can be seen in other examples of their work. There are some inconsistencies here, however, with clouds and rocks occupying the same levels. Nevertheless, their attention to detail means that interpreting the extant fragments is much easier than might be expected; and it becomes entirely possible to discern what the composition of the Keele window represents. Stylistically the fragments provide enough evidence to enable the conclusion to be drawn that the window glass is an example of international Gothic glass painting favoured in the century after 1250.

A centrally placed crocketed canopy in a setting of vine leaves, for instance, clearly indicates the presence of the figure of a single saint at the centre of the image. A painted golden crowned head with an elaborate stellar crown points to this being a representation of an exceptional individual, namely The Blessed Virgin Mary herself, as Queen of Heaven *(Regina Coeli)*. The use of pot metal yellow here to achieve a golden effect in representing the Virgin is early and may indeed be the earliest example of its use in this way in England. It certainly pre-dates its use at York Minster, for instance[18] and, even now, is striking in its luminosity in certain lights.

[Fig. 16: The golden crowned head of the Virgin as *regina coeli*, is an early example of the use of yellow stain produced by painting silver oxide on to white glass. Here, besides cumulonimbus clouds and rocks, one separately leaded panel depicts what could possibly be interpreted as a representation of the moon, which is otherwise missing from the scheme at Keele (lower right).]

[18] J. H. Harvey, 'Architectural History from 1291 to 1558' in *A History of York Minster*, ed. G.E. Aylmer & R. Cant (1977), 155, & D.E. O'Connor & J. Haselock, 'The Stained and Painted Glass' in *ibid*. 350; Alexander & Binski, *Age of Chivalry*, 137-8.

In fact, the image of the Virgin in the Keele window is the key to the identification of the subject matter of the entire scheme, which is a physical representation of a verse from the Book of Revelation:

> *'And there appeared a great wonder in heaven; a woman clothed with the sun, and the moon under her feet, and upon her head a crown of twelve stars'*

Revelation,12, v.1[19].

---

[19] *Et signum magnum apparuit in caelo: Mulier amicta sale, et luna sub pedibus eius, et in capite eius corona stellarum duodecim.*

[Fig. 17: *Revelation* 12, v.1: the sun and Virgin's head crowned with twelve stars.]

In the early middle ages, this verse was taken to refer to an unnamed virgin, the personification of the Church. During the twelfth century the Assumption of the Virgin gained popularity as an iconographical image as devotion to the Virgin, the universal mother, became more specific and replaced cults of local saints of often questionable sanctity.

From the twelfth century, however, as Marian theology evolved, it came to be identified with the Virgin Mary herself. What we have at the centre of the window at Keele is therefore a representation of the Assumption of the Virgin, the most important celebration of the Virgin Mary in the Christian calendar. It was an image that grew in popularity throughout the later middle ages and, for example, locally, this is demonstrated in the fifteenth century Assumption image depicting the Virgin with a *mandorla* at Gresford Parish Church in Clwyd, with the sun and moon here shown as projections on the Virgin's clothing. Images of the Assumption follow a standard pattern with only small variation wherever they occur. Hence Titian's wonderfully colourful treatment of the subject over the High Altar of the Dominican Friary in Venice (1516-18) is merely a sophisticated and realist Renaissance version of what survives at Keele, painted more than two centuries later.

At Keele, therefore, not only do we have the crowned image of the Virgin, but we also have, as part of the Assumption scheme, a fine depiction of the sun (here located almost immediately above the Virgin's crown), shown in a style which closely resembles the image of the sun in the Bodleian Library's Douce Apocalypse, a manuscript made to celebrate the marriage in 1254 at Burgos in Castile of the Lord Edward – the future Edward I – with Eleanor of Castile, sister of the Castilian king. The image of the moon appears to be missing at Keele, although one ambiguous and tantalising, separately leaded fragment towards the foot of the window could possibly be an attempt to indicate the lunar body, which, in England, is usually shown at this period as a crescent moon in half the image and a human face in the other, as in the fourteenth century window of St Michael and All Angels at Heydour (Lincolnshire). As at Keele, this also has a six-pointed flaming sun.

[Fig.18: Keele: Typical thirteenth-century representation of a flaming sun in the style of the Bodleian Library's Douce Apocalypse.]

We do, however, have here clear representations of the rocks from which the Virgin ascended, indications of the azure blue of the sky and images of the clouds, cumulonimbus, through which the Virgin passed. Other than her golden head and crown, the figure of the saint herself is, unfortunately, missing, except for some fragments, both in the main body and in the mouchettes, indicating her clothing and revealing that she is wearing a bright green gown, probably a cote-hardie, as suggested by the folds seen in one of the mouchette fragments[20].

[Fig. 19: Upper part of right hand mouchette with a fragment of the Virgin's green *cote-hardie.*]

[20] Another stained glass image of the Virgin wearing green was in the parish church of Hadzor (Worcestershire) and is now in the Museum of Stained Glass at Ely, *Age of Chivalry: Art in Plantagenet England, ed. J. Alexander & P. Binski* (1987) no.740, p.534.

By comparison with contemporary manuscript representations of The Assumption, the Keele image is very simple, and early. As Peter Newton pointed out, cycles of the Virgin are rare in the English Midlands, and extremely unusual in glass and, where they do occur, as at Newark and Gresford, they tend to be fifteenth-century phenomena. There are two further representations of scenes from the Virgin's life of a similar date in Staffordshire churches, but these are of particular episodes – a Virgin and Child at Checkley and a Coronation of the Virgin at Church Leigh, and both are considered to be by the Coventry school of glaziers. Of about the same date, the Ramsey Psalter (c.1300), now in the Pierrepoint Morgan Library, comprises three scenes depicting the death of the Virgin, angels assuming her to Heaven with Mary in a mandorla, and the crowned Virgin with accompanying saints. This arrangement is typical of the early fourteenth century. The contrasting simplicity of the Keele image indicates that its principal purpose was to celebrate the Virgin herself and to place her within the political context of the revived crusades.

The upper registers of the window to the left and right of the central canopy depict images of architectural structures, truncated and re-arranged crockets, finials, pinnacles and towers, seemingly cut down in scale from a larger original window light, but clearly indicating substantial church buildings on the one hand, and more secular castle-like structures on the other. The intention of the designer is to give an overwhelming impression of a crowded city and highly active building operations.

This is Jerusalem – the new Jerusalem, that will follow hard on the proposed crusade's successful recovery of the Holy Land. The restorers, Clayton and Bell, have clearly been particularly sensitive to the glass designer's original intentions and, although they have used glass fragments from elsewhere in their scheme, they have successfully conveyed the impression of urgency required. The elaborate treatment of the details here, however, suggests the design is of continental origin, as can be seen in the complex configuration of spires. The spires and spirelets with 'blisters' are not features found in English glass design

[Fig. 20: Keele's Templar window: Jerusalem rebuilt.]

of the period but have an affinity with continental exemplars. In fact, at Keele, this is not English glass, as we shall see.

The propaganda of the window is completely overt; the message contained here is that salvation is to be found only through a renewal of crusading and by contributing to the rebuilding of Jerusalem physically and figuratively. The theme is driven home by the depiction of two figures on a tower, facing away from each other, wearing the clearly identifiable dress of masons with specific trade-identifying headgear – flat caps. Each also has a small ruff, a very un-English garment at this period, but – probably intended to provide an element of personal protection to the wearer. The masons here are seen dressing stone and holding tools of their trade[21] – adzes and compasses are identifiable, in what is a very early and rare image of masons at work. However, these figures can, be identified as sergeants, lay brothers of the Order of the Temple. As such, they are unique[22], for the right-hand figure is wearing a tunic tied with a chord suggesting his membership of the Order. Here, therefore, we have the image of Templar stone masons standing in an open galleried tower building the New Jerusalem.

---

[21] J. Harvey, *The Master Builders: Architecture in the Middle Ages*, (1971), 12-14 discusses the changing meaning of the term 'mason'.

[22] cf. H. Nicholson, *The Knights Templar: A Brief History of the Warrior Order* (2010), 137.

[Fig.21: Keele's Templar window: representation of mozarabic tower.]

But where do these images originate? The architectural model in not English or even French, it seems, but hints at an Iberian origin. The tower from which the masons lean at Keele appears to have an architectural affinity with the tall towers of churches with open galleries found in the Pyrenees. Deep in the Upper Garonne valley, in France, for example, is Saint Aventin with similar galleries and there are other church towers like it in Andorra. Close by, just on the southern side of the mountain range we find the most likely architectural models for the Keele tower in Aragon. There are about a dozen churches with similar features situated here just to the south of the Pyrenees, such as the Benedictine foundation at Santa Cruz de la Seros, San Pedro at Larrede and San Miguel at Daroca. Just in Catalonia, stands the twelfth-century church of Sant Climent de Taüll in the Val de Boi exhibiting very similar features. In this valley, there is a group of eight eleventh- and twelfth-century Romanesque churches with similar design characteristics, including tall belfries, often six storeys high, identified as Lombardic in origin, and all with external decorative schemes similar to that depicted in the Templar window at Keele. What, at a glance, appears to be a classical influence in the image of a tower at Keele, is now clarified by these closely related sub-Pyreneean examples. The tower in Keele's window is a Romanesque structure in the Lombardic style imported to Catalonia and Aragon from Italy, but with distinct mozarab influences also apparent – and the glazed window itself containing the image of a galleried tower was brought to Keele by the pro-Aragonese Grand Master of the Templar Order, Jacques de Molay, in the last decade of the thirteenth century.

[Fig.22: Catalonia: Sant Climent de Taüll is one of eight similar churches in the Val de Boi with tall belfries and external decorative motifs.]

This is not as fanciful as might at first seem likely, for, although he was born a Burgundian, at Beaune in about 1265, Jacques de Molay's patron appears to have been James II, king of Aragon, with whom he worked closely on Templar and Aragonese affairs[23]. The Templar commandery at Gardena, near Lerida, was an active administrative centre for the Aragonese Templars from the mid-twelfth century, and the order had several commanderies in the Ebro valley. In 1220, the closeness of the Templars to the Aragonese crown was re-emphasised when the Order appointed chief accountants to the administrations in both Aragon and Catalonia[24].

It is not surprising, therefore that after de Molay became Grand Master of the entire Templar Order in 1292, he surrounded himself with Aragonese advisers previously in the service of the Crown of Aragon, who willingly stepped in to fill the void created by the loss of so many senior Templars at Acre in 1291[25]. Nor can it surprise us that when Jacques de Molay set out for his visit to England in 1293 he started from Aragon. It now seems fairly certain that the glass in the window at

---

[23] James was a minor on his accession in 1213, his care and custody being entrusted to the Templars (T.N. Bisson, *The Medieval Crown of Aragon: A Short History* (1986), 58.

[24] T.N. Bisson, op.cit, 32, 47-8, 60-1.

[25] A. Demurger, The Last Templar: The tragedy of Jacques de Molay (2005), 78-9.

Keele came from Aragon and was brought to England by, or on behalf of the Master of the Order of the Temple himself as a gift.

There was certainly no issue of capacity in Aragon. Glass furnaces were found there from Roman times, and in several locations. The earliest recorded evidence for glass making in Aragon dates from the 1180s when a local glassmaker was granted the privilege of taking all the nettles growing around the monastery of Poblet in order to secure a supply of sodium carbonate which could be extracted from nettles and was an essential ingredient of glass making. James II's father, Peter II (1196-1213) encouraged the craft by successfully extending the privileges of the craftsmen, to such an extent that by the early fourteenth century the city of Barcelona forbade the creation of further glass furnaces within its walls. Indeed, the evidence that Keele's window glass was made in the hinterland of Barcelona, in Aragon, can be seen in the window itself.

However, perhaps the most striking images in Keele's medieval window are those preserved in the parallel border friezes along either edge. They do not form any part of the general narrative carried by the central part of the window but provide a commentary on it by means of the symbolism of the images they present. The glass in the parallel friezes is also slightly later in date than the central panels of the window but cannot be later than 1307.

The two vertical friezes along each edge of the window contain a matching scheme of alternating lions' heads and ballflower/rosette decoration with smaller rosettes separating each head or large ballflower in the sequence – a scheme of sixteen images in total. Each head and larger rosette/ballflower is separately enclosed within a *vesica*, a shape creating a two-pointed oval characteristic of the late thirteenth century glass makers art, which can help to date the glass in which it features[26]. At Keele, there is an unusually extended surviving scheme with four complete painted lions' heads and two further part representations of them, although in heraldic terms they should probably be more accurately described as leopards in the armorial conventions of the period

[26] *Vesica*: a decorative device, deriving from the shape of a bladder.

since these lions are depicted full faced, *passant guardant*[27].

The lions' head device is a particularly interesting example of the work of the Chester glaziers. The image appears to have been inspired by the vision of St John in the Book of Revelation where the lion triumphant in these images is identified as Christ: 'the lion of the tribe of Juda, the Root of David'[28], and the image is also found in the Douce Apocalypse, the Lord Edward's own illustrated version of the Book of Revelation.

The glass painters responsible have interpreted the lions' heads slightly differently giving each an individual expression, from the quizzical to the comical, and by no means embodying the majesty that these symbols of Christ deserve. There is greater uniformity in the treatment of the large ball flowers and there are six of them representing the Virgin, each confined within its own *vesica*. The small ball flowers which originally

---

[27] The lions are probably heraldic leopards.

[28] *Revelation* 5,5.

[Fig.23: Keele - Chester glaziers' work- (i) lion's head from right hand frieze; (ii) ballflower rosette located immediately above the lion's head (left); (iii) lion's head top right from right hand frieze (iv) ballflower (bottom left) from left hand frieze.]

appear to have been intended to be in alternate blue and red roundels have suffered some discoloration through time so that several now have taken on a brownish shade.

The border friezes with alternating images of the symbols for Christ in Majesty and the Virgin Mary are English work, and, as previously stated, are the product of Chester glaziers, and can be identified by the appearance of the symbolic lions' heads in the decorative scheme which are a hallmark of these glaziers' work. The same device is found elsewhere in Cheshire and the North-West. At Nantwich Parish Church, a collection of six lions' heads have been gathered together in the south chancel clerestory.

[Fig.24: Nantwich parish Church south chancel clerestory; lions' heads with vesica. The window (c.1292) was commissioned by Robert Burnell, Bishop of Bath and Wells who was Edward I's chancellor and is another example of the Chester glazier's work.]

As at Keele they are distinguished by the use of the vesica as a decorative device, here rather less formal in shape than at Keele and they are undoubtedly of approximately the same late thirteenth-century date. This church was built to the commission of Robert Burnell, bishop of Bath and Wells and Edward I's Chancellor both before and after his accession, who died in October 1292. There are also single lions surviving in each of the two lights of the fine early fourteenth-century south chancel window at Tattenhall (Cheshire) celebrating saints Alban and Stephen, and there are others at Grappenhall (Cheshire) and at Halsall (Lancashire)[29] – all the work of the Chester glaziers who continued to use this particular device over a thirty-year period until at least 1320.

But why was the Keele preceptory the recipient of such generosity? There is little in the surviving record to suggest that this was likely, and modern historians, such as Professor Knowles and Dr Hadcock have been particularly dismissive[30]. In their seminal volume, *Medieval Religious Houses: England and Wales (1971 edn.),* Keele's foundation is said to be before 1255 - about eighty years later than now known to be the case - and 'was apparently a small house'. Their influential judgment, however, does not seem to fit the facts that

---

[29] P. Hegbin-Barnes, *The Medieval Stained Glass of Cheshire*, CVMA (2010).
[30] D. Knowles & R.N. Hadcock, *Medieval Religious Houses: England and Wales* (1971), 292; 294.

are now emerging, since Keele was a preceptory where admissions to the Templar Order took place, but it does account, at least in part, for the way in which the preceptory has been neglected, if not by the Grand Master of the Templar Order himself.

Jacques de Molay is known to have been concerned about the tarnished image of his Order after the events of 1291. The distribution of largesse was one way of counteracting the political damage done. The gift of the window to Keele fits with what we know of de Molay's political judgment and it was in line with what others did for similar reasons in the thirteenth century. The Grand Master repeated the gesture in 1295 with a parallel gift made to the Italian monastery at Torre Maggiore in Puglia, while another personal gift of his, was of a *castrum* - whether an encampment or castlery, is unclear - which was made to knights in the service of Pope Boniface VIII[31]. Gift giving was not unusual; the selection of Keele perhaps is, and we certainly need to wonder why.

---

[31] A. Demurger, T*he Last Templar*, 80.

Examples of gift giving were set by the royally connected in the thirteenth century. Beatrix van Valkenburg, the third wife of Richard, earl of Cornwall and king of the Romans, who died in 1270 was the earliest donor we know of in England[32], and the royal lead was soon followed by the wealthiest individuals of the day, like Peter de Dene, canon of York Minster, whose magnificent gift of the Heraldic Window in the Minster's nave, celebrates the chivalry of England and has the only representation in glass of an individual Knight Templar and, separately, a Knight Hospitaller. This window must therefore date from no later than 1310 and has recently been ascribed to the first year of Edward II's reign[33]. But, what is the date of the Keele window?

Various strands of evidence point the way. First, we know that as a commission by, or for, the Knights Templar, the Keele glass cannot date from after January 1308, when the order ceased to function

---

[32] Given to the house of friars minor in Oxford, it is now in the Burrell Collection in Glasgow (*Age of Chivalry*, no.226).

[33] *A History of York Minster*, ed. G. Aylmet & R. Cant, 349-50.

freely. In addition, the arguments used by Alexander and Binski to suggest a date for Peter de Dene's magnificent Heraldic Window in York Minster with its images of single knights of the Temple and the Hospital help us considerably. Their conclusion that, when allowances are made for the erection of this very large window, and a gap in the time between papal proscription of the Templar Order and the instructions to the glaziers being carried out is taken into account, the York Minster window cannot be later than 1310. This provides a useful reference point for dating Templar associated items and has hitherto provided the yardstick by which works associated with the Templars in England may be dated. However, we also know that at Keele, the sheriff of Staffordshire and Shropshire came to the preceptory in January 1308 to take it into royal custody, where it remained until 1324. No investment in the estate occurred in these years making it most unlikely that any variation in the circumstances of the former preceptory occurred and confirming that the window would have been in place by early 1308, at least three years earlier than Thomas Totty's interrogation at his trial. The Keele Templar window provides a further reference point for we now know that the Keele window is not related directly to the dissolution of the Templars but pre-dates that event. If we are correct to argue that the Keele window was set up as a consequence of Jacques de Molay's visit in 1293-4 and derived from a commission to glass makers in Aragon, then it follows that the window glass dates from those years, more than a decade earlier than other evidence has suggested.

Stained glass was very expensive, but it was an easy demonstration of status for the rich to donate in the manner of Peter de Dene. York Minster's Bellfounder's Window of the first quarter of the fourteenth century is another example, but this was the gift of a wealthy goldsmith and bellfounder of Stonegate, York, indicating the progression of gift giving from royalty to the merchant class by about 1325[34]. Jacques de Molay's gift to Keele, therefore, although smaller in scale than the York examples quoted, and earlier, shared the same mixed motives of generosity and self-aggrandisement, and in this instance, in particular, was

---

[34] *Ibid.*, 352-54.

intended to advertise the case for the newly proposed crusade.

It seems, however, that the Keele preceptory was treated uniquely in this way by de Molay. There is no evidence of other similar gifts to any of the other fifty or so Templar preceptories in England. It immediately raises the question, *'Why Keele?'* But any answer to that question is certain to be conjecture.

Perhaps, however, there were other reasons, now lost, or at best only hinted at in the record. Was Keele rather more significant in the English Templar hierarchy than is usually accepted? Probably not, the evidence suggests that the house was neither large nor small, nor particularly exceptional, although it does figure more frequently than might be expected in the record of the trial of the Templars in 1311. We learn that it was also a house where admissions to the Order occurred. Individual Templars with a Keele connection might also have been regarded as more important than the preceptory as a whole. Might there have been more personal reasons for the gift of the window for which no overt explanation now exists?

The role of Thomas Totty, certainly requires explanation, as far as that is possible, and will be considered later. He was, however, as we shall see, a shadowy figure and one of the most difficult of all the Templars to track in detail - which, almost certainly, is what the Inquisition intended. But he emerges from the record of the trial of the Templars as a larger than life figure, about whom the clerks of the Inquisition permit us to know only the sparsest of details. For instance, it is not until the very end of his evidence that we learn of his military and naval career as a Templar. Yet the trial seems to have given him the opportunity to suggest that there was more to him than the clerks of the Inquisition were likely to allow to be revealed. Much is not made explicit.

***

Jacques de Molay's journey to the west in 1293-4, on his first European venture outside Cyprus therefore had two main purposes. The first was essentially domestic and was intended to forestall proposals for a merger between the two major military orders being canvassed by the older established monastic orders such as the Benedictines and Cistercians. But the second, and more significant purpose, was to drum up support for the new crusade proposed by various popes and supported avidly by The Templars. It was also designed to encourage Edward I, who had failed to set out for the east, as promised, to overcome his reluctance to do so. It is intriguing to observe that Edward and de Molay could have been renewing acquaintance when they met in Acre in 1272. They shared a common experience and had a common purpose in a new crusading enterprise, and they met in London on 8 December 1293. Records show that they discussed outstanding issues concerning the operation of the Templar Order in England, with the clear suggestion that the Grand Master had already visited the Templar preceptory at Cressing in Essex as part of his general tour of English Templar houses to encourage support for the crusade.

Jacques de Molay's journey to the west in 1293-94 is sometimes cast as a spur of the moment decision. But the evidence suggests that it was better planned than that. The dimensions of the glass provided for the Keele window seem to conform to this interpretation. De Molay had spent his earlier career in Cyprus and was to return there after his stay in the west. Here several Templar churches existed, which the Grand Master would have known well. How did he know what size of window embrasure needed to be filled with his commissioned glass in England unless there was a roughly common scheme for all such Templar structures? His model is likely to have been a Templar church with which, we know, from extant records, he was personally very familiar, such as that still standing in Famagusta, which was his Order's headquarters in Cyprus.

[Fig.25: Famagusta Templar Church, apse window. The window is now blocked to enable projection facilities to be installed on the internal wall.]

The single light in the apse which occupies the east end of this Famagusta church is in the form of a lancet and appears to correspond fairly closely to what was thought to be required at Keele – except that, as we now know, the commissioned glass was too narrow for its embrasure and needed to be retro-filled by new glass on site provided by Cheshire glaziers. This explains why there are parallel friezes of lions' heads and flower designs at each edge of the Keele window. This glass was supplied by Cheshire craftsmen and with its characteristic thirteenth-century motifs was put in place at the same time, or, very shortly after the donated glass was erected.

Although a precise timetable is very difficult to construct from the information we have, Alain Demurger has provided a tentative programme for the Grand Master's visit to England, which shows clear evidence of advance planning for the journey[35]. De Molay did not travel alone but with a variable number of assistants, advisers, and servants. We do not know the names of his companions on his visit to England, but we know that his household comprised of at least one permanent chaplain and a clerk, a number of domestic staff, including a personal valet, a small military contingent, including a turcopolier, to act as an interpreter, as well as a senior officer in charge of the

[35] Demurger, *The Last Templar*, 78-80.

sergeant brothers of the order. We also learn that 'the guard of the bedchamber of the Grand Master overseas' was with de Molay for 'a year and a day' before he returned to the continent in 1294, but he is as anonymous as the rest[36]. Two Templar knights were also permanently attached to the Master's company, one from Provence and the other from Aragon[37]. Membership of the Master's household group was rather more fluid than might be suggested by this list, but there was an inner core of at least half a dozen who went everywhere with de Molay.

In 1293 the newly elevated Grand Master sailed from Cyprus early in the year and, appears to have travelled by way of Marseilles to Provence. From here he wrote to Edward I, asking for the Templar Master of England, Guy de Forest, to be permitted to attend a General Chapter of the Order due to be convened at Montpellier in August 1293, at which de Molay intended to be present.

---

[36] *ibid.*, 127.

[37] In 1293/4 these are likely to have been Raimbaud de Caron, who came from Provence, and Simon Exemen de Lenda, who was Aragonese.

The general chapter took place as planned but appears to have been interrupted by an urgent request from James II, king of Aragon, for de Molay to divert to the Iberian kingdom to complete negotiations between the Templars and the Aragonese kingdom for the transfer of Ruad, a small sandbank in the Mediterranean off Tortosa, two miles from the coast of Syria. This undoubtedly delayed the Grand Master's progress. Whether or not he made the journey through Roussillon and Languedoc in person, or took ship for Barcelona, or was represented by a member of his council, is also not known, but, it is at this point that de Molay, most likely, came into possession of, or commissioned, Keele's window glass.

Jacques de Molay was said to be in England to hold Chapter meetings of his Order which clearly indicates the itinerant nature of his visit, as well as his purpose in promoting the proposed crusade. The details of his English itinerary are unclear; we do not know when he arrived, or which preceptories figured in his itinerary, and in which order, or, precisely when he left the country. It is arguable that he had arrived in September

1293. The earliest reference to his presence in the country puts him at Garway (Herefordshire) in late November; that was the evidence given by the Templar chaplain, John de Stoke, at his trial in July 1311, when John is said to have been interrogated by the Grand Master in person. But dates lifted from the account of the trial of the Templars in 1311 are not certainly reliable due to the way in which the evidence was recorded, the unfamiliarity of the clerks of the Inquisition with English locations and the sheer terror of the witnesses from whom evidence was collected.

On 8 December 1293, when de Molay was recorded at Westminster, and met with the king, we are on more secure ground because the dating evidence comes from two references in Edward I's Patent and Close Rolls[38]. The substantive issue for discussion on this occasion was the behaviour of a former Master of the Temple in England concerning Cressing in Essex. Cressing was one of the wealthiest Templar preceptories with two huge barns for barley and wheat which are strongly indicative of the main purpose of the

[38] *C.P.R.,1292-1301*,56-7; close roll 54/iii/m.12.

Templar estates in England, namely raising supplies and cash to meet Templar needs elsewhere in Europe[39]. To the Master of the Templar Order in 1293, the wealth of Cressing and the content of its barns would have provided a measure by which to judge the likely success of the proposed crusade's appeal for funds. But what the Grand Master found at Cressing also presented him with problems.

The issue was the Templars' neglect, or ignorance, of the operation of the English Forest Law which had resulted in a claim of waste against the Order, a serious offence in England after the issue and subsequent confirmations of Magna Carta between 1215 and 1225, and its associated Forest Law of 1217. Two pieces of woodland in Cressing had been sold off and removed from the jurisdiction of the Forest by a former Master of the Templars in England without proper authority. They had therefore been seized by the crown. The Grand Master was clearly given a dressing down before the king instructed that both woods be restored to the possession of the Templars in a transaction which has

---

39 Essex County Council, *Cressing Temple: A Guide* (1997).

all the hallmarks of the renewal of acquaintance of two old friends. Yet these events give the impression that this was an expensive rapprochement for the Cressing Templars.

But, where else did de Molay go? The evidence is fragmentary and inconsistent. We know that there was an encounter with the Templar, John de Stoke which is said to have taken place at Garway on 30 November 1293, and that this was followed by the meeting with Edward I at Westminster in early December. From this it can be inferred that the Grand Master had already been at Templar properties in Essex. The following month, de Molay had reached Lincolnshire, first visiting the Templar preceptory at Eagle, a short distance south-west of Lincoln, and then, also in January 1294, he arrived at Temple Bruer, near Sleaford.

The preceptory here was a very substantial structure with a circular nave, and was named from the Latin after the gorse heathland on which it stood. It was the richest Templar house in England after The Temple in London, making its fortune from the raising of sturdy Lincolnshire sheep. The fact that Bruer figured in his itinerary demonstrates how precisely the Grand Master targeted his fundraising activity. It was here that de Molay chose to hold a chapter meeting of the English Templars, no doubt, to make the case for support for the crusade. It was a reasonable decision; there was a

[Fig.26: 'The North View of Temple Bruer…' (1726), from Samuel Buck's, *Buck's Antiquities*: indicating the extent then still standing of the circular nave of the preceptory.]

greater concentration of Templar houses in this county and in adjacent parts of Yorkshire than anywhere else in the kingdom.

Our knowledge of de Molay's itinerary in England is especially disappointing since a principal reason for his journey to the country was to encourage fellow Templar brethren to renew their crusading endeavours after the disaster at Acre. There are tantalising hints of the detail of his journey, but the evidence is never explicit. Temple Dinsley (Hertfordshire) is mentioned in the trial evidence of Brother Ralph of Barton in 1311, but it is not at all clear that this preceptory figured in de Molay's travels.

We can surmise that as de Molay moved through the country he maximised his opportunity to visit other Templar foundations. The houses visited in 1293 were the wealthiest Templar preceptories, but it is, nevertheless, a very thin record that has survived. It is a similar story for de Molay's progress in 1294 and, in contrast to his treatment of Keele, there is no hint that any of these preceptories received any gift at all from the Grand Master. The Grand Master is likely to have visited Temple Balsall (Warwickshire), for example, but the evidence for such direct contact is entirely circumstantial, and but for the presence of its Templar window, we would have to conclude in a similar negative vein about Keele. There is no extant documentary evidence of de Molay's presence at Keele, yet the indications, from the window glass alone that he was at Keele, is strong.

But what was the date of his visit? The Templar's patron was the Virgin Mary and the principal subject of the Keele window is a visual representation of the Virgin's principal feast day, the Feast of the Assumption which falls on 15 August. Did de Molay intend to be present at Keele on the Feast of the Assumption to hand over, install or preside at a dedication of the window? If so. In which year, 1293 or 1294? There are problems with both suggested dates. For instance, if the Grand Master, attended the provincial chapter at Montpellier, which met in August 1293, for any time longer than a very brief stay and then travelled to Aragon, before setting out for England, it is unlikely that he could have made Keele by 15 August that year. In 1294 our knowledge of de Molay's precise itinerary is equally sketchy, as we have seen, but we know that he was preparing to return to Aragon during the summer of this year. Letters of safe conduct were provided for him by the Aragonese king - but letters of safe conduct do not provide hard and fast evidence of a date but are merely indicative of intent; they do not permit any conclusion to be drawn as to when de Molay left England or travelled elsewhere.

The earliest confirmed date for his having left England is 27 August 1294 when he had arrived in Lerida in Aragon. If it was his intention to be present at the presentation of his window gift to the Templar preceptory at Keele, how possible was it for de Molay to have been at Keele on 15 August and in Lerida just twelve days later?

With a supply of fresh horses, he might just have made it, but it was a journey of several hundred miles involving a sea crossing of the Channel and then the lengthy land crossing of France and a pass through the Pyrenees. It would have been difficult in the time available in 1294. It is, therefore, unfortunate that we have no clear indication of whether de Molay made it to Keele for the Feast of the Assumption in either 1293 or 1294. On balance, it seems that 1293 is more likely to have seen de Molay on the road to Keele rather than 1294 – but we cannot, on present evidence, be sure.

On the other hand, it is quite possible that, although the subject matter of the window is a celebration of the feast of the Assumption, another date favoured by the Templars could have served and fitted in to de Molay's known itinerary rather better. Alain Demurger has pointed out that the Templars also used the feast of Saint John the Baptist (24 June), as a day favoured for their Chapter meetings[40]. Our detailed knowledge of de Molay's itinerary in 1293 and 1294 is simply insufficient to enable closer identification to be made. What is certain is that the window dates from de Molay's visit to Keele and that, if the evidence from the trial of the Templars in 1311 can be relied upon, it was certainly in place in the Templar chapel at Keele in 1296.

Jacques de Molay's visit to England in 1293-4 was primarily intended to drum up support for a new crusade but also served as a tour of inspection of the Templar's properties in England. Given that the cost of

---

[40] A. Demurger, *The Last Templar*, 80-1.

hosting de Molay's retinue as he made his way around the country would have been a considerable burden on each preceptory, and that each Templar brother interviewed in 1311 was asked specifically whether he had encountered the Grand Master on his journey to England, it is amazing how few direct references there are in the records of the Templar trials to the places de Molay visited only thirteen years earlier. The inquisition's clerks clearly did a thorough job in minimising the significance and detail of de Molay's travels.

By the late summer of 1294, the Grand Master of the Templar Order had left England to return to Lerida. His attention now focussed on arrangements for the exchange of Tortosa (Ruad) off the coast of Asia Minor with Peñiscola in Valencia. In December 1294 de Molay was in Naples where a papal conclave met to elect a new pope following the abdication of Celestine V. While in southern Italy de Molay received a papal grant of the Benedictine monastery of Torre Majore and, in celebration of this donated another window to a favoured institution. The Grand Master of the Templars subsequently travelled to Rome for the coronation of the new pope, Boniface VIII, on 23 January 1295[41].

Jacques de Molay's journey to England had proved a very limited triumph. The movement intended to bring about a union of the two major military orders was successfully obstructed by the Grand Master of the Order. Although he had carried out a visitation of a number of English Templar preceptories, as he had intended when he set out in 1292, de Molay had not been able to secure the degree of either popular or political support that he had anticipated would be forthcoming for a renewal of crusading. The support of Edward I was crucial; he was the only European leader of the day of sufficient stature with personal experience of crusading and with a reputation which could be called upon to encourage others to participate. But the king prevaricated and promised action which proved undeliverable. Although there was some interest in reviving the crusades in England in the later thirteenth century, it was limited in scope and

---

[41] A. Demurger, *The Last Templar*, 80.

never of sufficient volume to encourage the notion that it might be successful, even with papal blessing.

Plenty of folk across Europe continued to make plans for the recovery of the Holy Places, but they were mainly dreamers rather than practitioners and de Molay's efforts came to nothing. Jacques de Molay must have been deeply disappointed by the state of the Templar Order in England which had just short of sixty preceptories in the country at the end of the thirteenth century, but, although there were numerous corrodians and other dependents in most Templar houses affiliated in some degree to the Templar Order, the membership of the entire Order comprised fewer than three hundred professed brethren. This demonstrates the fundamental weakness of the Templars in the early fourteenth century. The Order was ripe for rationalization. Although the French king turned on the Templars in the most dastardly of ways, there was certainly a strong case for root and branch reform by 1307; but this is precisely what de Molay was determined to resist.

At Keele, the Templars continued undisturbed, for more than a decade after Jacques de Molay returned to the continent with time to enjoy, to venerate, and to rejoice in their new window.

4

Thomas Totty and the Templar Window

The Templars in France had their fortress headquarters in Paris just to the north of the Seine but very close to the royal palace in what is now the Marais district of the city. Here they maintained what, by the last decades of the thirteenth century had become the office of receipt for the revenues of French crown. Consequently, the French Templars had become exceedingly rich. Providing money and banking services for crusaders in general, and for the French crown in particular was a lucrative business, but it had its downside. The Templars were envied for their success in money management but were loathed as moneylenders and as royal tax collectors in equal measure. To a royal administration burdened by the expense of historic debt, foreign war, internal conflict and dynastic aspiration, the Templars seemed to offer a solution for the French king and his administration's financial problems.

On 14 September 1307, Philip IV, issued his infamous letter addressed to all royal officials in the kingdom of France informing them of 'a detestable crime, an execrable evil, an abominable work, a detestable disgrace, a thing almost inhuman...' which had been reported to him concerning the Templars. So heinous was the alleged offence that royal officers were instructed to prepare to arrest all Templars in the kingdom. A month later the order was given, and the Templars were now, for the first time explicitly accused of denying Christ, spitting on the cross, indulging in acts of obscenity and of sodomy. It was a complete travesty; Philip IV had become the first victim of his own royal officers' propaganda which resulted in concocted charges of such gravity that the consequence would be the universal condemnation of the entire Templar Order and result directly in the confiscation of their property and wealth. The pope, Clement V, was easily convinced of the threat posed to the Christian order by the trumped-up charges. His king was persuaded; Clement was a Frenchman himself, a former archbishop of Bordeaux, and had been Philip's nominee for the office. On the other hand, Edward II demurred.

In October 1307 he wrote to Philip, and then to other European monarchs asserting the Templars' honourable standing, stating that they were an order 'constant in the faith' and had 'publicly borne the cross of Christ'.

Nevertheless, in November 1307, Clement V issued a bull ordering the arrest of the members of the Order of Knights Templar throughout Christendom, and, in England, despite his reservations, the instruction was confirmed by Edward II on 10 January 1308. Days later, the local Staffordshire and Shropshire sheriff's officers seized the Templars' lands and goods into royal hands. A local Staffordshire knight, William de Stafford, appointed as a keeper of the peace for the crown, formally took possession of the three Templar houses in the two counties, at Keele, Lydley Heys and Stanton Long and, with the assistance of the preceptor in each location, drew up inventories of their goods and chattels.

The Templar brethren attached to these houses in January 1308 probably thought they had seen it all before, for it seemed they were being treated as members of an alien priory - a convent, that is, with a mother house on the continent which would often be taken into the royal hands in spats between the English and French crowns. It would only be a matter of time before normal relations were resumed. There was, in any case, only one Templar brother resident at Keele after November 1307 - Ralph Tanet, who is described in the record as preceptor of Keele, except in one revealing instance where he is called 'deputy preceptor' suggesting that he was regarded as standing in for the official office holder. Ralph Tanet was not a knight, but a sergeant/serving brother of the Order. His duties were straightforward - service to the senior members of the Order and running his preceptory effectively. There is no evidence that he was unduly disturbed by the events of January 1308. Presumably he was confident that the charges being levelled against his Order would be shown to be baseless, and there is nothing in surviving records relating to Keele to show otherwise. At this point only the Master of the Templar Order in England, who was taken off to the archbishop's prison in Canterbury, and a handful of others were detained. Most were released in May

1309. In England, in 1308 there were few indications of the problems to come for the Templars.

Ralph Tanet was permitted to remain in place at Keele and given the standard allowance for displaced Templars of fourpence a day. According to the sheriff's accounts for his tenure of the Templars' estates, the allowance was paid for 264 days until Michaelmas 1308, and renewed for a further 88 days until 27 December. Roger Trumwyn accounted for the custody of Keele until 5 January 1309 but the accounts of his successor, John L'Estrange of Ercal, as sheriff, are incomplete and do not permit us to know whether Ralph continued on his books. As we know that Templars elsewhere were paid their allowance until 30 September 1309 it seems very likely that Ralph went on receiving his fourpence a day until that date. We know that he remained on the estate at Keele, during this period.

There were, however, clear signs of a growing impatience with the stagnation which had set in in dealing with the Templar issue. The papal bulls proscribing the Templar Order were given renewed publicity by repeating the French king's charges against it. In the absence of confiscated Templar land at this stage, Edward II sought to exploit potential income from the patronage attached to presentation to former Templar livings. But he went much further in the summer of 1308 by ordering significant quantities of supplies of wheat, barley, oats, peas, beans, as well as 300 pigs to be sent from the three Templar estates in Shropshire and Staffordshire to the Scottish March to support his campaigns there. The demand was harsh and bore little relation to what those estates could produce. The pope too was losing patience as no confessions of guilt to any of the allegations lodged against them had been made by any English Templars to date. In France there had already been many. It is not difficult to explain the difference. Torture was permitted in France both by the state and by canon law to secure confessions. In England the necessity had never been tested and was alien to local practice.

The decision of the pope, in the summer of 1309, to appoint inquisitors to hear cases in England, Scotland, and Ireland was a challenge to royal authority but, in the circumstances was very difficult to resist. The inquisitors duly arrived in September and the Inquisition sat for the first time in England in October 1309, presided over by Dieudonné, abbot of Lagny and Sicard de Vaur, papal chaplain and a canon of Narbonne cathedral. Their arrival was followed by orders for the Templar brethren from the northern province to be moved to prison either in York or in Lincoln, or, if their house was in the southern province, to the Tower of London. There they were to await examination by the Inquisition and a panel of English bishops. As a consequence, 219 English Templars were arrested and relocated. Ralph Tanet, preceptor of Keele, was moved to London and detained before the end of October.

Tanet was joined by forty-two other brethren examined by the Inquisition in the church of Holy Trinity the Less in the city. Here he was confronted by a questionnaire containing the same 87 articles of accusation brought against the Templars in France. In spite of the length and detail of the inquest, frustratingly for the Inquisition, no confessions were forthcoming from any of the forty-three, so that their inquisitors now turned to the Canterbury Provincial Council and to Edward II to request the use of 'ecclesiastical methods' to secure the admissions they sought. Once again, they failed, and the inquisitors complained in June 1310 that no one in England could be found to carry out the tortures effectively.

In May and June 1310, in France, dissatisfaction with the progress of the case against the Templars was to surface in the most grotesque fashion. These were perilous days to be a Templar. On 12 May fifty-four Templar brethren were loaded in carts, taken to a field outside Paris and summarily burnt to death, even while the case against them was still being heard. Four days later four more perished in an identical way. Nine more died at Senlis while the bones of a former Treasurer of the Order were disinterred and flung into the fire. More Templars were subsequently executed in Paris. Those awaiting examination by the Inquisition from this point onwards lived lives of utter panic both in France, and in England, where news of the French Templars' fates soon became known[42]. In front of the Inquisition fear

---

[42] M. Barber, *The trial of the Templars* (1978), 156-8.

and terror tied the tongues of many, which were unloosed only by the threat of the use of torture.

One of the Templars threatened in this way in England was Thomas Totty. Totty was a Yorkshireman from Thoraldby in Bishopdale, which lies only a couple of miles due east of the Templar preceptory at Penhill. Totty seems to have possessed a particularly dynamic personality, and certainly one in contrast to the majority of his Templar colleagues. For reasons which will become clear, he is, nevertheless, one of the most difficult of the brethren to pursue in detail, not least because, however irrepressible he was, the inquisitors seem deliberately to have set out to minimise his impact and his role in events. Even his name is recorded inconsistently, sometimes appearing as Thomas of Thoraldby, or as Thomas Totty, or Stotty, and variants, even the Templar brother called Thomas of Frouby is identified as being Totty because Frouby is described as fleeing before the Templars were arrested in England. Totty's testimony is recorded as laconically as possible by the clerks of the Inquisition who, in accordance with medieval practice, have no care for chronology, or for providing dates. Their lack of care for creating an accurate record of names of places and of people, most of which were alien to themselves as clerks and to their commissioners alike, has been a constant source of difficulty for those seeking to use the records of the trials ever since. It becomes easy to attribute malevolence, trickery or deceit where none existed to those who failed to conform to modern concepts of acceptable behaviour. Nevertheless, Thomas Totty comes across in his trial evidence as something of a self-publicist. He deliberately lied on his first encounter with the Inquisition and was duly rumbled, so, even though he was frightened into telling the truth later, it is best to regard his evidence as requiring corroboration wherever possible.

Thomas Totty was included in 1310 in a group of twenty Templar brethren from the province of York incarcerated at Lincoln. He was already in trouble and is described as an apostate who had abandoned his order. The inference is that he did not belong with this group of Templars from the archdiocese, having moved away from his original house which is not identified. He comes across in the trial records as troublesome, but that conclusion may be no more than inquisitional bias. Members of the Inquisition had good cause, at least in their eyes, for treating Thomas Totty with both circumspection and disdain. But Totty was certainly resourceful. He had a useful familiarity with places in Europe from Iberia to Cyprus. Inevitably, as a Templar, he saw both military and administrative service, and both on land and at sea. At one time he claimed, plausibly, to have acted as gonfalonier, standard bearer, carrying the Templar banner in action launched from Cyprus off Tortosa and the small island of Ruad, probably in 1300, and he knew details, and disapproved, of how the Templar forces tended to stand aloof from the main action, leaving the troops of the king of Cyprus and crusading forces to fight their Saracen opponents without Templar assistance[43].

At their examination in 1310 other Templar brethren noted that Totty had abandoned his Templar habit

---

[43] Nicholson, *The Proceedings against the Templars*, 407, fn.48, thinks that Totty was about 32 years old at this point and so sufficiently senior in Templar ranks to act as standard bearer, but she doubts the veracity of Totty's account.

immediately after the arrest of the French Templars was known, and that he had adopted secular dress in the meantime. That would have been in the late summer or autumn of 1307; the date seems to coincide with the appearance of Ralph Tanet at Keele with the rank of deputy preceptor, but this cannot be conclusive proof that Totty had served as the senior Templar at Keele before absconding, because we know that

[Fig.27: Famagusta, Templar church: gonfalon rests for streamer banners. Thomas Totty served in the Templar navy off Cyprus as gonfalonier in the Order.]

others, unnamed, also abandoned the Templar habit at about the same time. It is, however both possible and, in the circumstances of his admiration for the Keele window as expressed in his trial, quite likely.

The arrests of the Templars were affected in France, on and after 13 October 1307. Between twenty and thirty brethren absconded immediately, but how soon was the news picked up in England? One of those absconding was the elderly, distinguished, Imbert Blanke, Grand Commander of the Auvergne, who had been received as a Templar at Tyre in the Kingdom of Jerusalem nearly forty years earlier, who now made his way across the Channel. Was he the informant of the English Templars who caused Thomas Totty to throw off his Templar identity?

It is possible, but Keele had already been deserted by its preceptor, before the sheriff's officers arrived to seize the Templar property there in January 1308, and most probably, as early as the previous September, when the first hints of French royal hostility towards the Order were manifested. As already suggested, this would provide an explanation for Ralph Tanet being called ‘deputy preceptor’ in the records at this point, and ‘preceptor’ in subsequent documents. If this is the explanation, was Thomas Totty the absentee preceptor of Keele? He was certainly shrewd enough to absent himself in the circumstances. Did he travel abroad, as he did later, or remain in England? We do not know, but he was not at Keele, and he is lost to view from the autumn of 1307 until he was incarcerated at Lincoln in 1310. Because his house was in the southern province, however, he was regarded as an interloper in the group. It is possible, and almost certainly the case, that he took advantage of the unusual concentration of Templar foundations in Lincolnshire, where there were at least six houses of the Order including Temple Bruer, and in Yorkshire, Totty’s home county, where there were a further eleven in which to seek safe refuge. His major problem at this stage was that because he had abandoned the house to which he had been admitted, he was now regarded as an apostate, and therefore outside the law.

Totty was never content to keep a low profile, however personally dangerous. Even before he could be brought for inquisitorial examination in Lincoln Castle, we know that he had bribed the sheriff of Lincoln and the constable of Lincoln Castle with forty gold florins to release him, 'for fear of death', he claimed, when confronted in 1311. This episode seems to indicate that he was a person of some clout, in his own right, with access to money and with the capacity to engage in such a course of action - but it was an extraordinarily risky strategy to adopt. Totty took his opportunity crossing to Europe, travelling to France and the Papal Court, then residing at Avignon in the south of France. In answers to questions from his interrogators in June 1311 Thomas stated that he fled from custody because of the personal intimidation he suffered at the hands of his inquisitor, the abbot of Lagny who, 'putting his hand on his breast swore by God's Word that he would make him confess before he escaped from his clutches'. That is why, he asserted, he had approached the sheriff of Lincoln and bribed him to allow him to walk away from Lincoln, not clandestinely, but in broad daylight. This incident is significant not only for suggesting that Thomas had personal means to fund his activities, which may be of relevance when considering how the

Templar window arrived in Keele, but because it demonstrates that English officials, such as the county sheriff, Ranulph of Rye, and the constable of the castle were not simply venal but had little sympathy for the novel legal processes being used against the Templars.

In his deposition Totty then tells us that he went first to the Roman curia, resident in Poitiers at this point, where he had an audience with the papal penitentiary – the curial official, most appropriate in the circumstances, appointed to hear confessions and to enjoin penances, and Thomas is at pains to tell us that this was not an independent initiative on his part but that the Master of the English Templars himself had licensed his journey, and had granted permission for him to travel in secular dress while on his mission on behalf of the Templar Order as long as he wore *'the mantle of his habit'* at all times. Totty was undoubtedly attempting to cover his back when he subsequently went to France where he hoped his secular habit would have disguised his Templar connection.

We have no further record of who he saw, who he contacted, where, precisely, he went, or, who accompanied him. Did he visit Aragon, or perhaps, Cyprus? It is suggested that he was on a mission for the Grand Master of the Order and these locations were a continuing focus of de Molay's concerns. This is mere conjecture, except to confirm Totty's apparent closeness to Jacques de Molay. Unsurprisingly, Totty found himself outcast as a fugitive, and excommunicated as a result of his venture.

Totty was at liberty until he surrendered himself on 25 June 1311. On the very next day, however, he was handed over to the ecclesiastical authorities in London for trial by the Inquisition. He had no satisfactory explanation for absconding from custody the previous year, except that, as he said, the threat to his life. Each of the three English Templars – Stephen of Staplebridge, John of Stoke and Thomas Totty – who had either absconded or failed to surrender in 1310, were now deemed to have confessed to heresy, and each of them was subjected to torture at some point in the proceedings against them.

When Totty was first interrogated in the Chapter House at Lincoln in April 1310 he had said that he had been admitted to the Templar Order at Keele twenty-eight years previously, that is, in 1282. It was fanciful, if the inquisition clerks recorded him accurately. Was the claim an error, terror, or complete deceit? His deposition and demeanour suggested his intention to be evasive and the Inquisition was not to be fooled. It meant he would be re-examined under duress. His second examination took place on 24 and 25 June 1311 in the church of St Martin Vintry in London and, after torture, continued four days later in the prior's chamber in the Augustinian house of St Mary Overy, in Southwark[44]. Whether it was a result of compulsion, or of the oath he swore to tell the truth on this occasion, Totty's answers had a ring of truth about them that was absent earlier. Totty now told his inquisitors that fifteen or sixteen years before, and at about the Feast of the Assumption, he had been received into the Order at Keele in the diocese of Coventry and Lichfield by the Grand Commander of the Templars in England. This was on, or about, 15 August 1295 or 1296, exactly one or two years since The Grand Master of the Order,

[44] M. Barber, *The Trial of the Templars*, 201-2.

Jacques de Molay, had been present there himself. Inadvertently, in this submission, we learn that the Keele preceptory was of altogether more significance within the Templar Order than has been generally assumed. Here is the evidence that Keele was of sufficient stature, to be a place where admissions to the Order took place and was a location at which major office holders among the Templars in England would assemble.

For Thomas Totty, however, a lengthy interrogation, euphemistically styled a 'confession', followed. Its details are very informative, but, of particular interest, was the demand that Totty should renounce the Virgin Mary, and his negative response. The text requires quotation:

> 'Also, they endeavoured to compel him to deny the Blessed Virgin Mary, and to spit over her image, but neither did he wish to do

this, on the contrary, he kissed the feet of the image, as he said'.[45]

Requiring him to renounce the Virgin was a challenge to Totty's loyalty to his order since all Templar houses were dedicated to her, while spitting on her image challenged his attachment to his house, which the context indicates was Keele. Although mediated by the Inquisition's scribes, and intended to present a hostile anti-Templar stance, this chapter of his confession contains a clear reference to the newly erected window in Keele's Templar chapel, with its representation of the Assumption of the Virgin, which enables us with certainty to date it to before 1311. But we now know, from other evidence, that we can be more precise and state that it dates from the last decade of the thirteenth century. It is remarkable and perhaps a testimony to Totty's personal skills, that his utterance about kissing the Virgin's feet was allowed to stand in

---

[45] *Item nitebantur eum conpellere ad negandum beatam virginem Mariam, ad spuendum super ymaginem ipsius, set nec hoc facere voluit immo osculabatur pedes ymaginis ipsius, ut dixit'* (*The Proceedings Against the Templars in the British Isles,* ed. Helen J. Nicholson (2011), *Vol 1: The Latin edition*, p.355; Vol.2: *The Translation* (2011), p.405.)

[Fig.28: The fragment of the Virgin's green robe preserved in a mouchette (above) and her golden head (below - Fig.29) are the only certainly identifiable representations of the Virgin in the window.]

the summary minutes of the proceedings against him, for it is the Virgin's image which survives and is at the centre of Keele's medieval window still, that adds so much credence to Totty's responses at his trial. The double use of the term 'image' in this section is significant, for it is made clear that a physical object is being spoken of. That Totty was in awe of the window is also clearly evidenced by the inquisition clerk's formulation of the entry. Stained and painted glass was a rarity in the 1290s outside major cathedrals, so that it is difficult, for us today, in our age of visual surfeit, to comprehend the wonder expressed by the setting up of painted and stained-glass images in medieval chapels and parish churches. Before the mid-fourteenth century when the opportunity to view such wonders became much more commonplace, the effect of their luminosity on the viewer could be very powerful and completely entrancing. Even today, at Keele, the sheer brilliance of the golden head of the Virgin in the glass in certain lights is a very moving spiritual experience.

Even in adversity Totty appears to be expressing pride in his Order but especially in his house. Keele was certainly a focus of his affection. That was probably because he was admitted to the Templar Order here, but also because he had an especial devotion to its image of the Virgin. Although we cannot answer the question definitively we need to ask whether this suggests that Totty had a personal role in the importation of Keele's Templar window. It seems very likely and Totty's evidence to the Inquisition can also be used to fix a date for the erection of the window at Keele for, if Thomas Totty's assertion is correct that he was received into the Order of The Temple at the feast of The Assumption of the Virgin, 15 August in 1295/6, and that on this occasion he kissed the feet of the Virgin, and if, as contended, his confession contains a reference to the Keele window, it means that the Keele window must have been in place by August 1295/96. Thomas Totty may have been acting in adversity when before his inquisitors, but he appears to have been shrewd enough to get them to reveal sufficient of his interrogation to point up his own views of his situation and to manipulate some of the evidence presented in his favour.

So finally, in this section, what more can be said about whether Totty was the absentee preceptor of Keele who quit his post before 1308, leaving Ralph Tanet, a sergeant of the Order, not a knight, in charge in its final years? There is no direct evidence to confirm it, but it seems likely, and some corroboration is offered by the record in the Staffordshire sheriff's accounts for the confiscated preceptory indicating the presence of a Templar knight's surcoat in its inventory of the order's possessions at Keele in 1308. It seems unlikely that this belonged to Richard de Bonington, preceptor at Keele in the 1270s and the only known named preceptor before this date. It certainly did not belong to Ralph Tanet for he was not a knight, while Totty's military exploits certainly suggest that he was. Could this be the Templar garb that he discarded in around 1307? He is an intriguing character whose inquisition record raises many issues because of the censorship practised by the Inquisition but he leaves a distinct impression that his doings are everywhere understated. He had no control and little influence on how the inquisitors reported on him, but it did.

What is particularly noteworthy about his 'confession' is that the image, whose feet Totty kissed, survives in part in the parish church of St John the Baptist at Keele, hitherto unrecorded. It is a significant piece of evidence concerning the last years of the Templars in England.

5

Survival – Thomas of Lancaster

The seizure of the Keele estate in the king's name in 1308 by officers of the sheriff of Shropshire and Staffordshire marked the start of a very sharp decline in the fortunes of the Keele preceptory and exposed the manor of Keele to the predatory financial inclinations of a monarch and administration hard pressed to meet its military commitments in Scotland. Its resources were plundered by the crown in 1308 and its manorial equipment and stock was sold off to support Edward II's abortive Scottish campaign.

Worse was to follow, when the Templar estate was illegally seized by the overmighty and regally connected Earl Thomas of Lancaster, who falsely claimed it as part of his own lordship of the manor of Newcastle-under-Lyme. It was a preposterous claim and a land-grab that could only have been made at a time when the crown itself was so exceptionally weak. Keele had been given to the Templars by King Henry II as a reward for loyal service in the Angevin cause, and because of the papal concession to the Templar Order in the early twelfth century, the manor and its tenants were exempt from control by all except the pope and his legates. Newcastle, on the other hand, was re-founded as a new royal castle and borough on land, originally held by the earl of Chester, in the north of Trentham manor, and was taken back by the crown after the accession of Henry II in 1154. They were, therefore, distinctly different political entities, but that did not matter to Thomas, earl of Lancaster when laying claim to Keele in 1312. In these years, the earl was politically untouchable, so that the effect of his claim to Keele was to freeze the lordship in political aspic.

Thomas was the son of Edmund Crouchback, Edward I's younger brother and was the first cousin to the king, Edward II. He was also the holder of five of the eleven English earldoms – Lancaster, Leicester, Derby (Ferrers) acquired from his father, and Lincoln and Salisbury from his wife. As *de facto* challenger for the monarchy itself during Edward II's reign he was irresistible in his lifetime, and quickly gained a reputation as a grasping and voracious landlord. For example, the *firma burgi* of Newcastle-under-Lyme, paid by Newcastle burgesses, was raised by a third at a stroke from the forty marks a year fixed by Thomas's father, Edmund Crouchback, to forty pounds (£40) by Thomas, while Lancaster's attempts to raise cash from his tenants caused them to complain of the earl as a grasping financial operator[46].

In 1312, after the suppression of the Templar Order, the pope ordered the transfer of former Templar lands to the Knights Hospitaller and in most instances, this happened without event. The Templar estates at Keele should, therefore, have passed to the Hospital at this point, but this did not happen. The earl was determined to retain them for himself and used his political power to prevaricate and stonewall. The Knights Hospitaller were never sufficiently strong enough to be able to challenge Lancaster's behaviour and therefore never secured Keele in the earl's lifetime. As a result of his imperious behaviour, Earl Thomas was able to keep the Hospital at bay for the rest of his life 'being of higher

[46] T. Pape, *Medieval Newcastle-under-Lyme* (1928), 57-8; J.R. Maddicott, *Thomas of Lancaster, 1307-1322* (1970), 39n.

birth and more powerful than the rest', to quote the chronicle, *Vita Edwardi Secundi,* commenting on Thomas's role in the killing of Piers Gaveston in 1312. The chronicler then goes on to re-enforce his view by explaining that not only was Thomas the nephew of Edward I, and therefore of royal birth, but that, as the son of the Lord Edmund, and the holder of those five earldoms, he was not to be gainsaid. Worse, the Keele estate, to which he had no lawful title, was systematically asset stripped by the earl.

Earl Thomas was executed for rebellion against the king following his defeat at the Battle of Boroughbridge in 1322, but still the Keele estate was kept out of the hands of the Hospitallers. Lancaster's lands, including Keele, were decreed to be forfeit to the crown as the estate of a contrariant, and it was another two years before the Hospital was able to acquire it, a full decade after the papal instruction to hand it over. But, by then, it was too late for them to rescue it, because, in addition to Lancaster's aggressive defence of his illegal acquisition, the economic woes of the first two decades of the fourteenth century had taken their toll. The severe agrarian crisis of the period 1314-21 had a particularly devastating effect on Keele when records show that tenants' rents proved uncollectable over several years and some holdings in the manor were completely abandoned. There was also a shortage of draught animals in these years meaning that crops could not be gathered in, and, between 1319 and 1321, a cattle murrain carried off many beasts. The Hospitallers' attempts to revive the impoverished manor failed very quickly and, by 1324 they had begun a process of leasing their holdings in Keele to local townsmen, merchants and others which continued for the rest of the medieval period. The former preceptory no longer functioned as an independent religious house, but became dependent on the Hospitaller establishment at Halston, which is situated between Whittington and Ellesmere in Shropshire.

But it was not all bad news in these years, for Keele's Templar window survived these vicissitudes. Lancaster's wilful misunderstanding of his authority in Keele was a factor. By arguing that Keele was part of his manor of Newcastle he challenged the exempt status of the Keele estate, at the very time that the pope confirmed the significance of exemption by deliberately protecting the exempt orders, the Templars and Hospitallers, from the attempts of jealous landlords and others to seize their lands. While other former Templar estates were often dramatically altered by the Hospitallers to make them conform to that Order's requirements, Keele avoided the changes wrought, for instance, at Garway, which resulted in the destruction of its original circular nave. Indeed, at Keele, the Templar structures, including the chapel and the Old Hall survived the middle ages, largely unscathed. It was only in the nineteenth century that the Templar church was pulled down on the orders of its Sneyd landlord in the 1860s. The Templar window, seemingly rather battered, neglected, and clearly misunderstood by its custodians was nonetheless preserved, repaired and relocated. Wear and tear had taken its toll on the window glass over time at Keele, but it allowed Clayton and Bell to stabilise what was left of it after 1868.

*****

The contents of Keele's Templar window are undeniably a piece of ingenious political propaganda intended to revive flagging enthusiasm for crusading against a background of the considerable difficulties and the expense of mounting crusades in the thirteenth century in general, as well as the disappointments of St Louis' two crusades, and, in particular, after 1250, the creation of a Mamluk sultanate in Egypt and Syria. By the 1280s the position of the crusader territories in the east was desperate and all but irretrievable. Their fate was finally sealed by the fall of Acre after a siege lasting from early April to mid-May 1291. How to re-engage with crusading ideals in these circumstances and how to enthuse local folk for a cause which necessitated such a long distant commitment were issues which pre-occupied popes and statesmen alike in these years. Undoubtedly Jacques de Molay, Thomas Totty and all who proselytised for crusading were doomed to failure in their support for a cause that had largely outlived its value by 1300. All the effort and all the enthusiasm which still existed in some quarters for a renewal of the crusades came to nothing in these years which

Jonathan Riley Smith has accurately summarised as campaigning for 'A Crusade that never was'[47].

For all its chequered history, the Templar window is a remarkable survivor - a very rare and probably unique link in England to the career of the last Grand Master of the Templar Order, Jacques de Molay, who brought the window as a gift to Keele in 1293/4 and who, in 1314, scandalously suffered the same fate as many of his French brothers. The destruction of the Order of Knights Templar is a tragic story which even in our own day, can have unfortunate misguided reverberations as the headline from a clipping from *The Loughborough Echo* of 2017 attests.

[47] Riley-Smith, *The Atlas of the Crusades*, 122.

TRADER WARNED PREVIOUSLY OVER NAZI ITEMS IS BANNED FROM

Coffee mugs declared offensive

The Knights Templar mugs declared offensive.

Report by Megan Cox

A LOUGHBOROUGH market stall holder, who previously appeared in the *Echo* defending her right to sell WWII books and memorabilia sporting swastikas and photos of Adolf Hitler, has now been banned from having a stand in the town centre after selling Knights of Templar coffee mugs.

But Charnwood Borough Council, which took the decision to ban the trader, says it can't "comment as to why the mugs were offensive".

The *Echo* reported in August that the borough council had intended to write to Tina Gayle, who has been selling predominately vintage books and history books at Loughborough market for almost three years, following "several complaints" about Second World War items "which could be deemed offensive to some".

And last Friday (October 6) she was further told she could no longer trade at any Loughborough market, as concerns had been raised about her selling Knights Templar coffee mugs.

Turn to page five

[Fig.30: Coffee mugs declared offensive – *Loughborough Echo* (2017) – comical, but a worrying manifestation of intolerance. (I am grateful to a Loughborough resident for sending me this clipping.)]

Further Reading

The Proceedings Against the Templars in the British Isles, 2 volumes (2011) ed. Helen J. Nicholson.

Age of Chivalry: Art in Plantagenet England, 1200-1400, ed. J. Alexander & P. Binski (1987)

M. Barber, *The Trial of the Templars* (1978)

M. Barber, *The New Knighthood: History of the Order of the Temple* (1994)

E. Burman, *The Templars: Knights of God* (1986)

Alain Demurger, *The Last Templar: the tragedy of Jacques de Molay* (2009)

A. Forey, *The Military Orders from the twelfth to the early fourteenth centuries* (1992)

Michael Haag, *The Templars: History and Myth* (2008) [is careful to distinguish the myth from the history]

P. Hebgin-Barnes, *The Medieval Stained Glass of Cheshire*, CVMA (2010)

Simon Lloyd, *English Society and the Crusade 1216-1307* (1988)

Christopher T. Maier, *Crusade Propaganda and Ideology* (2000)

Helen Nicholson, *The Knights Templar: A Brief History of the Warrior Order* (2001)

Jonathan Phillips, 'The Crusades', *History Today*, 65, May 2015 [provides a useful overview]

J. Riley-Smith, ed., *The Atlas of the Crusades* (1991)

R. Studd, 'Keele before the Sneyds' in *Essays on the History of Keele* (1986) ed. C.J. Harrison